AF604882

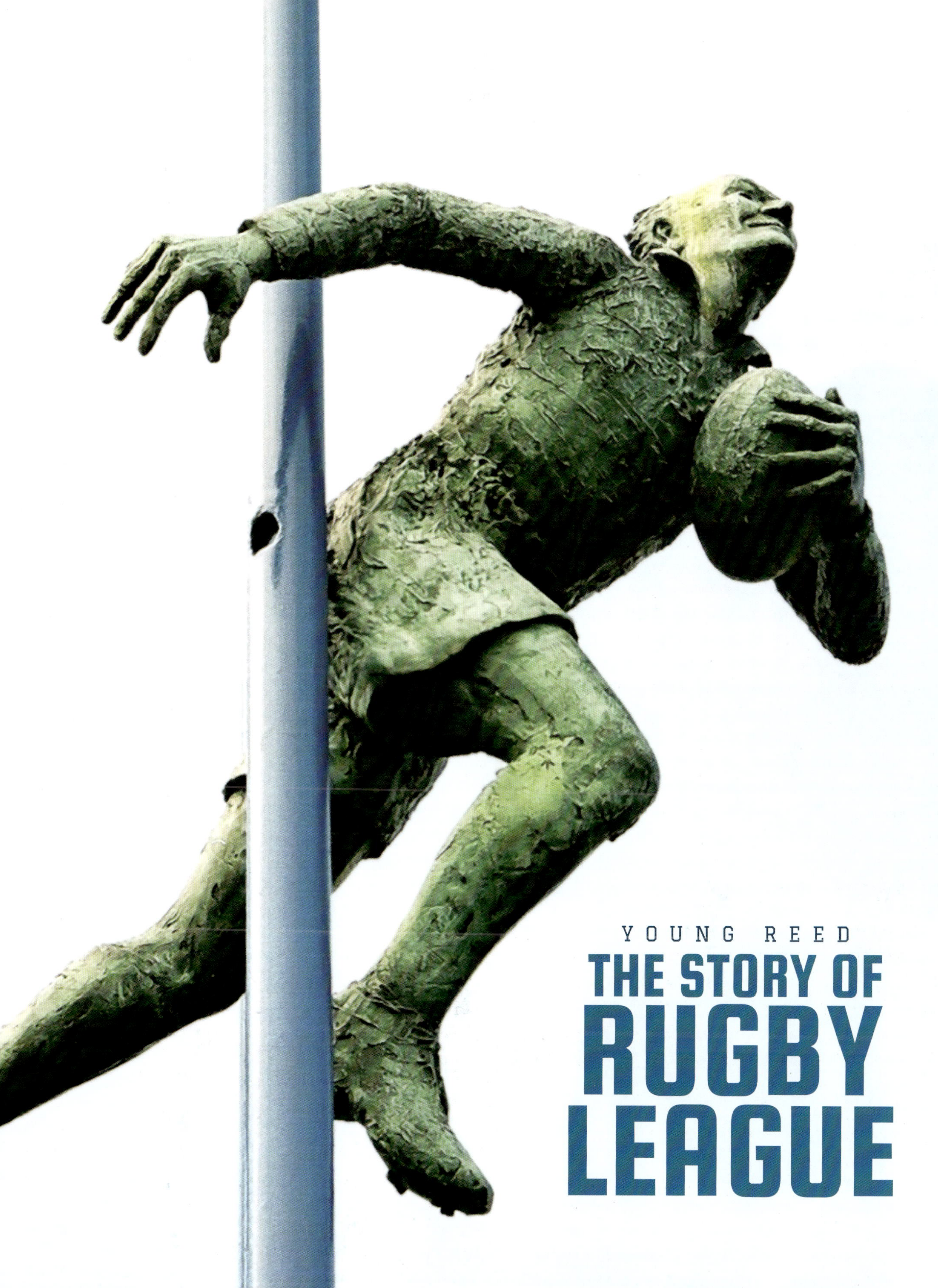

YOUNG REED

THE STORY OF RUGBY LEAGUE

First published in 2018 by New Holland Publishers
Revised 2019
This edition revised 2025

newhollandpublishers.com

Copyright © 2018 New Holland Publishers
Copyright © 2018 in text: Andrew Ferguson
Copyright in images Ian Collis, NHP files, public domain and AAP.

All rights reserved. No part of this publication may be reproduced, stored in a retrieval system or transmitted, in any form or by any means, electronic, mechanical, photocopying, recording or otherwise, without the prior written permission of the publishers and copyright holders.

A record of this book is held at the National Library of Australia.

ISBN 9781921580901

Managing Director: Fiona Schultz
General Manager: Olga Dementiev
Publisher: Alan Whiticker
Designer: Andrew Davies
Production Director: Arlene Gippert

Printed in China

Keep up with New Holland Publishers:
NewHollandPublishers
@newhollandpublishers

Front cover photos. left: Wally Lewis; *right:* Johnathan Thurston; *Back cover photo:* St George players carry captain-coach Norm Provan from a mud-soaked SCG after the 1963 grand final win against Western Suburbs.

YOUNG REED

THE STORY OF RUGBY LEAGUE

THE GREATEST GAME OF ALL SINCE 1908

ANDREW FERGUSON

young reed

Introduction

I was introduced to Rugby League at the age of eight after catching a glimpse of the game being played on TV one cold winter day. The following year, on my ninth birthday, my Mum gave me a copy of David Middleton's *Rugby League 1989–90* Yearbook and from that day on, a fan of the game, and its history and statistics, was born.

After many years writing, researching and analysing statistics, I became involved with Shawn Dollin's website www.rugbyleagueproject.org and together we have turned the site into a huge archive of Rugby League matches from all around the world.

It's a wonderful, physical, fast and exciting game. Fans everywhere since its birth have lived the many highs and lows of the sport and continue to follow it with the same vigour and passion as it continues to evolve into the future. The game has a rich and colourful past, many times controversial, which is still being revealed and researched to this day.

I hope you enjoy this book and get a taste of how the game has evolved into the sport we know and love today. Its been quite a journey!

Andrew Ferguson, 2025

Acknowledgements

I have several people to thank on my journey to writing this book. These people have all been mesmerised by this great game like I have.

Firstly, my wife Suzie and daughter Elle and son Darcy, my parents Jill and Ian and my wife's parents Bob and Purita. I would also like to thank Shawn Dollin, Will Evans, Terry Williams, Tim Costello, Bill Bates, Nick Tedeschi, Steve Williams, Marc Leabres and Terry Liberopolous who are all good mates that have helped me immensely as I became a writer. Thanks also to Andrew Voss, Steve Mascord, Andrew Marmont, Ian Heads, Sean Fagan, Roger Grime, Tony Adams, Geoff Armstrong and Martyn Sadler for their assistance over the years.

A huge thanks to Olga Dementiev, Andrew Davies and everyone at New Holland for all their magnificent work in making this book a reality. Most of all I'd like to thank Alan Whiticker who has been a huge supporter of mine and has been instrumental in helping me finally write a book of my own.

Bibliography

A Short History of Rugby League by Will Evans
Pioneers of Rugby League by Sean Fagan
Retro Rugby League by Ian Collis
Rugby League Through the Decades by Ian Collis and Alan Whiticker
The ABC of Rugby League by Malcolm Andrews
The Finals: 100 Years of National Rugby League Finals by Steve Haddan
The Kangaroos by Ian Heads
True Blue by Ian Heads
The Encyclopedia of Rugby League Players by Alan Whiticker and Glen Hudson
Rugby League Review magazine
Sydney Morning Herald archives
www.rugbyleagueproject.org
www.leagueunlimited.com

ADVANCE
AUSTRALIA
GLEBE
NEWTOWN
SYDNEY
W. SUBURBS
EASTERN
SUBURBS
NEWCASTLE
BALMAIN
N. SYDNEY
CUMBERLAND

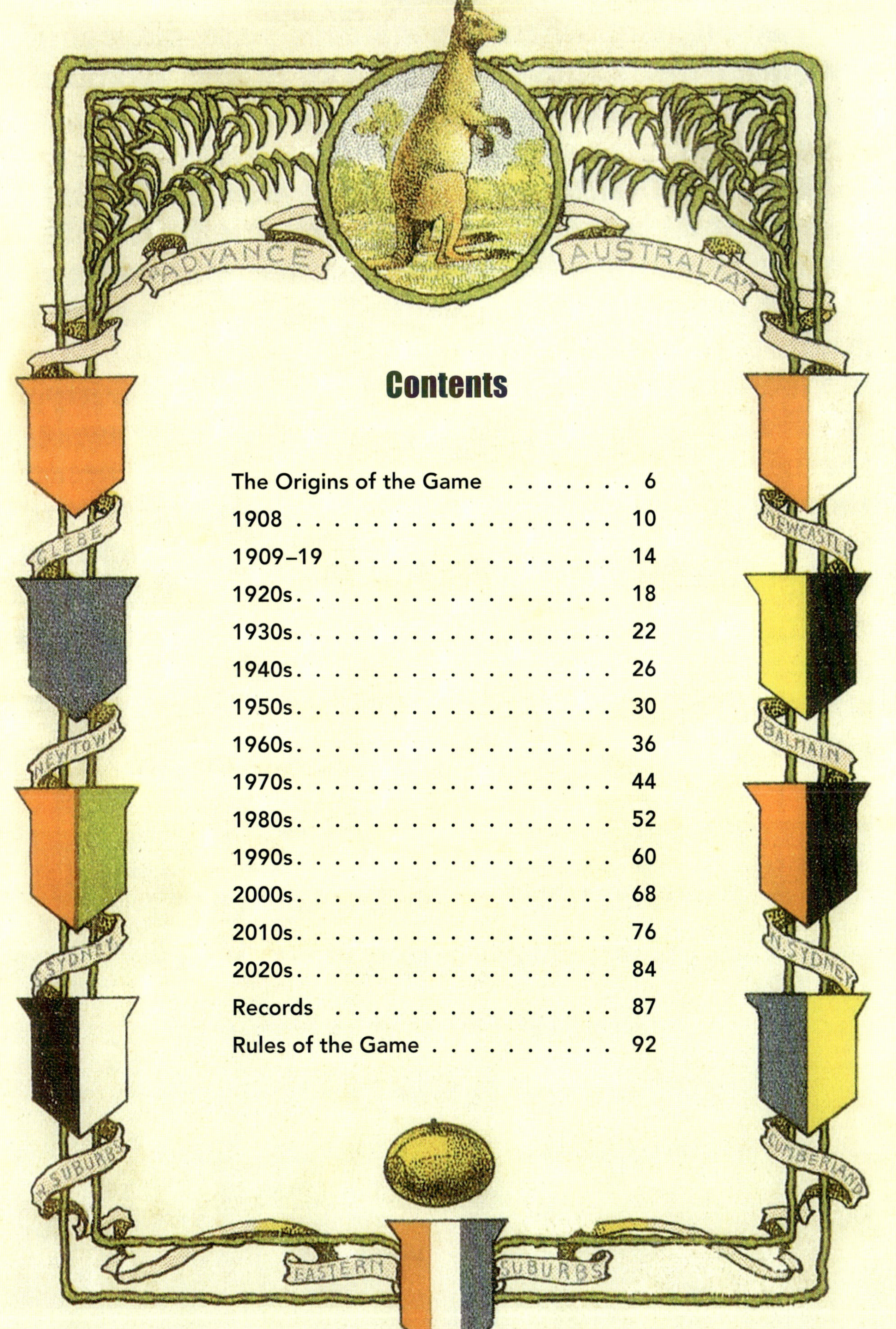

Contents

The Origins of the Game

Rugby Union was an outgrowth of a disorganised, free-for-all form of football played at English board schools in the early 1800s. Legend has it that in 1823, Rugby student William Webb Ellis 'with fine regard for the rules of football at the time' tucked the ball under his arm and ran with it. In one single act, or so the story goes, he had revolutionised the game of 'Rugby'.

By 1871, the rules of the game had been refined enough for it to be an established amateur football code in English schools. So popular was the game that it soon defied class boundaries and clubs sprung up in industrial areas of Northern England, intent on playing with the 'Rugby Union'.

The controversy that arose towards the end of the 19th Century, however, concerned the compensation of players who were injured in games played in working class areas and missed work. In 1895, at the George Hotel in Huddersfield, 20 teams from the north of England decided to break away and formed a rival 'Northern Union'.

Originally, the only difference between the two 'unions' was the 'professionalism' of the Northern Union game. If players were injured and could not work they would be paid from gate receipts for 'time lost' at work. But over the next decade, the rules began to change too and the breakaway code became known as the 'Northern League' or, more popularly, 'Rugby League'.

Above: Boys playing football at Rugby School, 1870.
Below: George Hotel, Huddersfield, venue of the breakaway meeting.

Rugby Union in Australia

The amateur Rugby Union code was first played in high schools and universities in Australia in the 1860s. By the turn of the century, Rugby was attracting hundreds of thousands of paying spectators each year but all the money was going to the Metropolitan Rugby Union or district clubs – not to the players. The first Test series against England was in 1892, and New Zealand played their first Test series in 1903.

In July 1907, popular Sydney player Alec Burdon dislocated his shoulder and was ruled out of that year's representative matches. To make matters worse, Burdon was a barber in the inner-city suburb of Glebe and could not work his job. The old argument of compensating injured players for 'time lost' at work was openly discussed in Sydney's sporting circles.

Just as importantly, however, the manner in which the Metropolitan Rugby Union ran the game and distributed gate receipts led to businessmen such as cricketer Victor Trumper, labour official Henry Hoyle and entrepreneur James Giltinan to consider backing a 'rebel' competition played along the lines of the Northern League's 'professional' Rugby League.

Above: Victor Trumper, master cricketer and entrepreneur.

Below: The New South Wales 'rebel' team, 1907.

The Coming of Baskerville's 'All Golds', 1907

In 1907 Albert Baskerville, a 25-year-old postal clerk in Wellington, New Zealand led a squad of Kiwi Rugby players to England in order to play a number of 'professional' Rugby League games. The group of former 'All Blacks' were labelled 'All Golds' by the media because they would be playing for money.

Disgruntled members of Sydney's Rugby fraternity suggested that the New Zealand 'All Golds' stop in Sydney on their way to England and play games against a hastily chosen NSW team. Sydney businessmen guaranteed the 'All Golds' £500 (about $70,000 in today's money) to play three games in Sydney and then went about luring high-profile Rugby Union players who were unhappy with the way the game was being run. Any player who joined the rebels was banned for life from playing Rugby Union.

By far the most important signing was that of Herbert 'Dally' Messenger, who was a superstar of the game before the word was even invented. Other top players quickly followed his lead and the three games, played under existing Rugby rules because no-one knew the League rules, drew a combined total of 100,000 people. The All Golds won all three games and then asked Messenger to go with them to England!

Above: James J. Giltinan, the Sydney businessman who financed the fledgling 'professional Rugby' competition in Sydney in 1908 – and finished broke! *Right:* The official souvenir of the New Zealand 'Rugby football' team that travelled to England to play the professional 'Rugby League' teams in 1907–08.

Albert Baskerville's New Zealand 'All Golds' in 1907. Baskerville is sitting in front holding the ball. On his left is the great 'Dally' Messenger who also travelled to England with the team.

The Birth of the New South Wales Rugby Football League (NSWRFL), 1907

On August 8, 1907 at the Bateman's Crystal Hotel in Sydney, at least 50 men, mostly Rugby players, attended a meeting which was to be the formation of the New South Wales Rugby League. The new League attracted some good Rugby players but needed a 'superstar' to ensure public interest in the new game. The 'League-ites' signed the most exciting Rugby player at the time – 'Dally' Messenger – thereby guaranteeing the code's success the following year.

1908

The First Rugby League Clubs

Glebe
Est. January 9, 1908

Newtown
Est. January 14, 1908

South Sydney
Est. January 17, 1908

Balmain
Est. January 23, 1908

Eastern Suburbs
Est. January 24, 1908

Western Suburbs
Est. February 4, 1908

North Sydney
Est. February 7, 1908

Newcastle
Est. February 10, 1908

Central Cumberland
Est. 21 April, 1908

1908 Final
Souths 14 • Easts 12

Did You Know?

The Cumberland (Parramatta) club was formed after the inaugural season had already begun and folded at the end of the year!

The first NSWRFL competition, 1908

Eight teams originally joined the League for the first season in 1908: Balmain, Eastern Suburbs, Glebe, Newcastle, Newtown, North Sydney, South Sydney and Western Suburbs. Players had to turn out for the team representing the region in which they lived, known as the 'residential rule', a system that was also used in cricket. This rule was in place for more than 50 years.

The first official games of Rugby League took place on April 20, 1908. Eastern Suburbs defeated Newtown 32–16, South Sydney defeated North Sydney 11–7, Balmain defeated Western Suburbs 24–0 and Glebe defeated Newcastle 8–5.

Three weeks later a ninth team entered the competition, called Central Cumberland.

Above: Sid 'Sandy' Pearce played hooker for the Roosters until he was almost 40 years old!

Above: The premiership winning South Sydney team which won the inaugural title in 1908.

The Rules of Rugby League

The rules of the game in 1908 were very similar to Rugby Union. League had 13 players, Union had 15; tries were reduced from four points to three, and all goals were worth two points. The ruck formed over a tackled player in Union was replaced by a 'play the ball' in League and instead of a sideline 'throw in' when a ball went out of bounds, League had a scrum.

Rugby League, like Union, was also played under the 'unlimited tackle' rule – that is, a team could keep the possession of the ball until a player lost it in a tackle. If a scrum penalty was given, a team could kick for goal. In the early days, if a player caught the ball on the full – like an AFL 'mark' – a team could kick for goal.

The First Finals

The finals system in the initial years of the game saw the top team on the ladder play third placed, and second play fourth. The winners then played in a final. Before the completion of the 1908 premiership season, however, many of the game's best players were selected to travel to England as part of the Australian Rugby League squad – 'The Kangaroos'.

On 29 August, South Sydney won the first ever premiership final, 14–12 defeating Eastern Suburbs, with both sides missing their star players. Because both Easts and Souths were even on 20 competition points heading into the final, South Sydney's win took them to 22 points, making them the inaugural premiers.

1908

Interstate Rivalry Is Born!

On July 11, 1908, the first game between New South Wales and Queensland was played. Queensland were still organising their own Rugby League competition at the time, which meant they fielded a side not fully prepared for the new game. The Blues won the game, 43–0.

A week later a second game was played with NSW naming a weaker side while Queensland was boosted by the selection of Newcastle star Pat Walsh. NSW won a much closer battle, 12–3, but more than a century of interstate rivalry was born!

Above: Pat 'Nimmo' Walsh who played for both NSW and Queensland in 1908.

DALLY MESSENGER: 'THE MASTER'

Born in Sydney in 1883, Herbert Henry "Dally" Messenger was a star Rugby Union player before switching codes to play the 'professional' game. Messenger toured England with the 1907–08 New Zealand side, returned to Australia for the 1908 season to play with Eastern Suburbs before returning to England with the 1908–09 Kangaroos. He stepped down from Test football at the end of 1910 and won a premiership with Easts in 1911. At the end of 1912 he decided to retire but was persuaded to play for one more year. After picking up his third straight premiership with Easts, Messenger retired from the game.

The 'Dally M' Medal for the NRL's 'player of the year' is named after him. In 2008 he was named in the ARL 'team of the century'.

Right: The great 'Dally' Messenger who was the game's first 'superstar'.

The Return of Baskerville's 'All Golds'

On April 22, 1908, just two days after the game officially began in Australia, the New Zealand 'All Golds' returned to Australia. They played another 10 games before returning home to New Zealand, including a 3 Test series against Australia, which they won. Sadly, tour leader Albert Baskerville caught a cold and died in Brisbane, aged just 25.

Two days after the Third Test, a New Zealand Maori team played their first ever game on Australian soil against NSW, going down 18–9. Their tour lasted two months, with 13 games played including another Test series.

Above: The Pioneer Kangaroos toured England in 1908–09 wearing the colours of sky blue (NSW) and maroon (QLD) and played the first 'Ashes' Test series.

The First Kangaroo Tour to England, 1908–09

In August 1908, 35 players were selected to play for Australia on a tour to England. They set sail from Sydney on August 15 and arrived in London on September 27. To stay fit, the players would shovel coal and do exercises on the deck every day.

They then played a total of 45 games in England, Wales and Scotland. The tour was great experience for the players but a financial failure, with workers strikes and bad weather keeping people from attending games. At the end of the tour, there wasn't enough money raised to buy fares home for all the players, so several stayed in England playing for clubs there instead.

After their return home, the game's founding father James Giltinan was sacked from his role as NSWRL Secretary. It was later reported that the tour of England had bankrupted him.

1909–19

The Premiers

1909 Final
Souths def Balmain (forfeit)

1910 Final
Newtown 4 • Souths 4*
* Newtown won on countback

1911 Final
Easts 11 • Glebe 8

1912
Easts (No Final Played)

1913
Easts (No Final Played)

1914
Souths (No Final Played)

1915 Final
Balmain (No Final Played)

1916
Balmain 5 • Souths 3

1917
Balmain (No Final Played)

1918
Souths (No Final Played)

1919
Balmain (No Final Played)

Team Changes
Newcastle left at the end of 1909.
Annandale entered in 1910.

Did You Know?

From 1912 to 1925 the team who finished the season in first place was awarded the Premiership. A final was only played if two teams were equal on the table.

Balmain forfeit the Final, 1909

After the financial failure of the 1908–09 Kangaroo tour, the League needed money for survival. Sir James Joynton-Smith came to the game's assistance and in a bid to lure star 'Wallaby' Rugby Union players to the professional code three games were played between the Wallabies and Kangaroos. The League's debt to Joynton-Smith was still not cleared, so a fourth game was scheduled on the same day as the premiership final between South Sydney and Balmain.

Balmain protested this decision on game day and refused to play the match. South Sydney kicked off against non-existent opponents, scored a try and were awarded the premiership.

Rugby League then secured the services of most of Rugby Union's greatest players, including captain Chris McKivat, which helped the game grow in popularity the following year.

The 1910 Final finishes in a draw

In 1910, the finals system of the previous two years was scrapped and replaced by a final between the top two sides. Newtown ended the season on 23 points and South Sydney were on 22. They played a hard-fought final that saw no tries scored and the scores locked at 4–all at full-time.

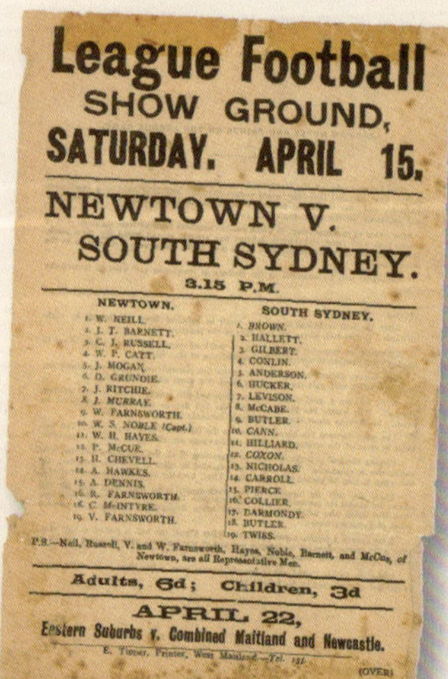

Officials then ruled that Newtown be awarded the premiership because of their higher position on the League ladder.

Two Finals! 1911

Glebe finished the 1911 season on 22 points while Eastern Suburbs and South Sydney were even on 20 points. These latter teams then had a match to determine which side would be the opponent for Glebe in the final.

Eastern Suburbs defeated South Sydney 23–10, with 'Dally' Messenger scoring 20 points for his side.

Easts then beat Glebe in the final, 22–9, which meant both sides were now even on 22 premiership points. A second final was played, which Easts won 11–8 to take the title of premiers.

Balmain, Undefeated Premiers, 1915

In 1915, the Balmain 'Tigers' went through the season undefeated, winning 12 games and drawing two matches. The club's reserve grade and third grade teams also won their respective competitions that year. All three Balmain grades repeated this feat in 1916 and the Tigers won again in 1917.

Below: The champion Balmain team which won a third straight premiership in 1917. As a result, the club was allowed to keep the premiership trophy, the 'Hugh D. McIntosh Shield'.

1909–19

1909: Rugby League competition begins in Brisbane

On May 8, 1909, Rugby League competition began in Queensland, despite heavy criticism from the media and the local Rugby Union. It came about after many players who wanted to play Rugby League and earn money had left the state to go and play in Sydney. The Queensland Rugby Union banned those players who made those journeys, but it had little impact.

With the Queensland Rugby League up and running, even more players changed codes, bringing Rugby Union in Queensland to its knees very quickly. The League in Queensland focussed on rural and regional areas as well as working class suburbs in Brisbane, areas which are still the heartland of the game today in the state.

1910–1914: 'Ashes' Test series against England

In 1910, England made their first tour to Australia and New Zealand, drawing sell-out crowds regularly. The Lions won the opening two Tests before losing to a selected 'Australasian' team that included three New Zealand players. The home team won one and drew the other match.

The following year, another 'Australasian' squad travelled to England where they secured a surprising Ashes series victory on enemy soil. This squad was led by the former Rugby Union player Chris McKivat.

England returned to Australia in 1914, winning back the 'Ashes' series after another successful tour. The series was tied one game all going into the Third Test in Sydney. The Lions lost three players to injury, with the rules of the day preventing replacement players coming onto the field. England won the game with just ten men in what became known as the 'Rorke's Drift' Test.

Below: Queensland, 1911. *Opposite:* England, 1910.

World War One: 1914–1918

The end of the 1914 season saw the start of World War I. The off-season provided much debate in Australia as to whether sports should abandon their competitions. Rugby League chose to continue playing in order to provide community relief from the misery of war. This decision drew a lot of criticism from the public and other sporting codes, most notably Rugby Union which chose not to play games.

Edward Larkin (1880–1915).

Many Rugby League players enlisted to serve in the War which impacted on the quality of all the teams playing stocks. Many star players, as well as League secretary Edward Larkin, lost their lives in battle. Rugby League also saw it had a great opportunity to raise funds for the war. Many exhibition games were played, where all the gate takings were donated to the war effort.

1919: The first tour of New Zealand

Australia made their first tour of New Zealand after the 1919 season where they dominated their opponents. The Kangaroos played four Tests against the Kiwis and won the series 3–1, as well as five other tour games against local outfits. Australia was led by champion halfback Arthur Halloway, who was known as 'Pony' because of his small size.

Right: Arthur 'Pony' Halloway.

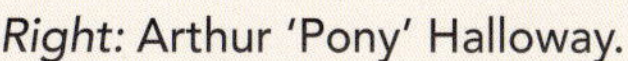

1920s

The Premiers

1920
Balmain (no final played)

1921
Norths (no final played)

1922 Final
Norths 35 • Glebe 3

1923 Final
Easts 15 • Souths 12

1924 Final
Balmain 3 • Souths 0

1925
Souths (no final played)

1926 Final
Souths 11 • University 5

1927 Final
Souths 20 • St George 11

1928 Final
Souths 26 • Easts 5

1929 Final
Souths 30 • Newtown 10

Club Changes

University entered in 1920.
Annandale left the League after the 1920 season.
St George entered in 1921.
Glebe left at the end of 1929.

Did You Know?

Round 5 of the 1924 season saw the unique situation where Wests captain 'Tedda' Courtney played alongside his son, Ed. This feat has never been repeated.

Women in Rugby League, 1921

In 1921, a new first for the game took place when two women from North Sydney, Molly Crane and Nellie Doherty, organised the first official game of women's Rugby League in the world. The proposal was initially met with mockery. However, after realising the ladies were not only serious but well-organised, determined and genuinely skilled, the League agreed to hold the game. On September 17, a game between Metropolitan Blues and Sydney Reds took place, with the Blues winning 21–11. Maggie Maloney scored four tries in front of the crowd of 20,000.

Above: A cartoon from *The Rugby League News*, June 1921

J. C. Ives — C. Blinkhorn. — H. Horder. — D. F. Thompson. — H. Peters.

NORTH SYDNEY RUGBY LEAGUE FOOTBALL CLUB.

A WELCOME-HOME SOCIAL

will be tendered to Messrs. H. Horder, D. F. Thompson, C. Blinkhorn, J. C. Ives, and H. Peters (members 1921 Australasian Rugby League Tourists)

ON TUESDAY EVENING, MARCH 7th, 1922
IN THE MANRESA HALL, CARLOW ST., N.S.

First-class Orchestra — Light Refreshments.

TICKETS 3/- plus tax

L. B. SCHOLFIELD, Hon. Treas. — J. L. DARGAN, Hon. Sec.

The Great North Sydney teams, 1920–22

After making the finals in their first season, North Sydney had a run of 12 straight seasons where they failed to reach the top four.

Everything changed in 1920 when their star-studded team won the State Cup and then won the next two premierships.

In 1921, Norths finished the season undefeated and champion players in their distinctive red and black jerseys included Test stars Cec Blinkhorn, Harold Horder and Duncan Thompson. The club won the title again in 1922, blitzing Glebe 35–3 in the Final. As it turned out, these would be the only 1st grade titles Norths ever won before the club exited the game 77 years later.

The Great Toowoomba Team of the 1920s

After his controversial suspension for kicking (which he denied) in 1923 while he was still at North Sydney, Duncan Thompson returned to his home state of Queensland and joined Toowoomba. They very quickly became a dominant Rugby League force defeating Ipswich three times; Victoria 47–18, NSW 16–0 and Great Britain 23–20 – all in 1924! Toowoomba were undefeated in 1925, picking up two wins over Brisbane, two wins and a draw against Ipswich, a 16–14 victory over New Zealand and a 12–5 win over the undefeated South Sydney side in a match described as the 'Club Championship of Australia'.

Above: A souvenir 'Duncan Thompson pin'.
Below: The great Duncan Thompson.

DUNCAN THOMPSON

Duncan Thompson was regarded as one of the smartest Rugby League players to ever play the game. A 1st grader at age 17, he debuted for his state just three years later against NSW.

Thompson signed with North Sydney in 1916 but at the end of the year he joined the Army where he was shot while fighting at the Battle of Dernancourt, with the bullet lodged in his chest.

He returned to the game in 1919, playing for Queensland and Australia. After spending 1920 in Newcastle, he returned to Norths in 1921 where he led the club to their maiden premiership title. After returning from the 1921–22 Kangaroo Tour he guided Norths to their only other title in 1922.

Thompson returned to Queensland in 1924 where he had continued success with Toowoomba and Queensland. He later coached Toowoomba to six titles in the 1940s and 1950s, and spent several years as an Australian Test selector.

1920s

South Sydney's great run, 1925–1929

After finishing as runners up in 1923 and 1924, South Sydney went on a magnificent run, winning five straight premierships from 1925 to 1929. In an unbelievable 1925 season, Souths won all 12 games and despite five rounds still to play, the 'Rabbitohs' were so far ahead on the ladder that the League ended competition early and awarded Souths the premiership!

In 1926, Souths played against Sydney University in the final, but the 'Students' lost 11–5. Souths then beat St George in the 1927 final, and Easts in 1928, before securing their fifth straight title with a 30–10 win over Newtown in 1929.

Above: South Sydney players Oscar Quinlivan, Jack Why, Harry Kadwell and Alf Blair, 1929
Below: The 1924 Final between Souths and Balmain.

The Internationals, 1920s

After the war ended, England returned to Australia in 1920 but were unable to retain the Ashes, losing the series two Tests to one. It would be the last time Australia won the Ashes until 1950. England won on home soil in 1921–22 and again, in 1924 and 1928, when they visited Australia.

The 1929–30 Kangaroos came very close to winning the Ashes. The series was tied one Test–all going into the decider. The Third Test at Swinton finished in a scoreless draw after Australia's Joe 'Chimpy' Busch was denied a seemingly fair try because the crowd came onto the field! A fourth game was organised which Great Britain won 3–0 to claim the series.

The Final, on radio for the first time, 1924

The shortened 1924 season saw just nine rounds of games played. Balmain and Souths played in the premiership decider that year, with Balmain winning a tough match, 3–0.

The match is notable for being the first ever game broadcast on radio in Australia. The broadcaster was Balmain Secretary Bob Savage, who called the game with all the bias of a one-eyed Tiger fan!

C.W. PRENTICE N.S.W.
R. VEST. N.S.W.
E. McGRATH. N.S.W.
R. TOWNSEND N.S.W.
F. RYAN. N.S.W.
W. RICHARDS QLD.
N. POTTER QLD.
F. BURGE N.S.W.
B. GRAY. N.S.W.
E.S. BROWN QLD.
N. BROADFOOT. QLD.
C. BLINKHORN N.S.W.
H. HORDER N.S.W.
D. THOMPSON N.S.W.
J.C. IVES. N.S.W.
H. PETERS N.S.W.
G. CARSTAIRS N.S.W.
S. PEARCE N.S.W.
H. CAPLES N.S.W.
J. WATKINS. N.S.W.
REX NORMAN N.S.W.
A. JOHNSTON. N.S.W.
L. CUBITT. N.S.W. CAPT.
S. GEO. BALL. Joint Manager.
1921-1922
W.A. CANN. Joint Manager.
C. FRASER. N.S.W. Vice-Capt.
AUSTRALASIAN FOOTBALL TEAM.
TOURING GREAT BRITAIN
R. LATTA. N.S.W.
W. SCHULTZ. N.S.W.
B. LAING. N.Z.
J. CRAIG. N.S.W.
MELBA STUDIOS 65 MARKET ST. SYDNEY

1930s

The Premiers

1930 Grand Final
Wests 27 • St George 2

1931 Grand Final
Souths 12 • Easts 7

1932 Grand Final
Souths 19 • Wests 12

1933 Final
Newtown 18 • St George 5

1934 Grand Final
Wests 15 • Easts 12

1935 Final
Easts 19 • Souths 3

1936 Final
Easts 32 • Balmain 12

1937
Easts (no final played)

1938 Final
Canterbury 19 • Easts 6

1939 Final
Balmain 33 • Souths 4

Team Changes
Canterbury-Bankstown entered in 1935.
University left after 1938 season.

Did You Know?

The 1937 season finished after just eight rounds because the game's best players had to go to New Zealand for a Test series before sailing to England on the Kangaroo Tour.

Wests captain Jim Craig kicking for goal in the first ever grand final, 1930.

The First 'Grand Final', 1930

In 1926, a new finals system was introduced, whereby the top four teams would take part at the end of each season. If the team who finished in first place on the ladder lost any finals game, they would get the right to challenge the winner of the final in what would be known as a 'grand final'.

1930 was the first time a grand final was played in Rugby League. Western Suburbs finished the year in first place but after defeating South Sydney in the semi-final, 9–5, they lost the final against St George, 14–6.

Wests then faced off against St George the following week, this time posting a convincing 27–2 victory to claim their first premiership title.

The Coming War, 1939

On September 1, 1939, the day before Balmain belted South Sydney in the League Final, 33–4, World War II began in Europe. Rugby League again chose to continue operating during the war, although this time the game faced much less criticism from society and other sporting codes.

Many League players again lined up to do their duty and serve their country. St George player Spencer Walklate served with a special elite force infiltrating Japanese bases in Papua New Guinea. He was killed on a secret mission in 1945.

Other Australian players who served during the war included Keith Holman, Les Cowie, Arch Crippin, Fred de Belin, Pat Devery, Edgar Newham, Roy Thompson and 1948 Test captain Len Smith.

The Great Eastern Suburbs Teams of the 1930s

The Eastern Suburbs side of the 1930s is still regarded as one of the most dominant in the game's history. The deeds of point-scoring wizard Dave Brown, hard and tough forwards Ray Stehr and Joe Pearce, and Test five-eighth Ernie Norman have become legendary at the club.

Easts' dominance of the 1935, 1936 and 1937 seasons is unrivalled in the game. They lost just one match in those three years. The team scored 633 points from just 18 games in 1935, the most points scored by a team in a season until their record was broken by Parramatta in 1982. The Eels scored 673 points but in 29 games!

Above: Former St George player Spencer Walklate.
Below: The champion Easts (Roosters) team, 1936

1930s

The Internationals, 1930s

England returned to Australia in 1932, winning the Ashes in the deciding Third Test. The 1933–34 Kangaroos were beaten in all three Tests by the brilliant British side.

Australia travelled to New Zealand in 1935, winning the first Test series between the two countries since 1919.

England returned to Australia in 1936, where they were dominated in the First Test but won the next two to retain the Ashes.

After playing a two-Test series against the Kiwis in 1937, the Kangaroos lost the Ashes series again in England. Australia then played their first ever Test series against France, winning both games in 1938.

Below: Australia and England, and various officials and pioneers, 1932.

Above: Canterbury-Bankstown players of the 1930s ... note the fashion!

Canterbury-Bankstown Join the League, 1935

Canterbury-Bankstown entered the competition in 1935 and had a horror first season in the League. In Round 5, they were on the receiving end of the biggest loss in the game's history, when St George beat them 91–6. The following week they were beaten 87–7 by Easts. Those two score lines are still the two biggest wins in the game's history.

DAVE BROWN, 'THE BRADMAN OF LEAGUE'

Dave Brown was known as 'The Bradman of League' due to his magnificent point-scoring ability. He made his debut aged 18 for Easts in 1930 and quickly became a crowd favourite with his bald head (Brown suffered from alopecia areata) and trademark headgear.

Selected on the Kangaroo tour to England in 1933–34, he scored a record 19 tries and 114 goals for 285 points. 1935 was his best season, however, setting records that still stand. Against Canterbury, he scored 5 tries and 15 goals for a total of 45 points in the 87–7 win. By the end of the year he scored 38 tries in 15 games and his total of 238 points was the most in a season until bettered by Souths' Eric Simms in 1969.

After leading Easts to the Premiership in 1936, Brown joined English side Warrington. After two seasons he returned to Easts before retiring in 1941 and spending the rest of his life working in League.

The following year Canterbury were an immensely better team, finishing the season in third place and reaching the finals. There were no finals in 1937 but incredibly, in only their fourth season in League, Canterbury defeated defending premiers Easts, 19–6, in the 1938 final.

1940s

The Premiers

1940 Final
Easts 24 • Canterbury 14

1941 Final
St George 31 • Easts 14

1942 Grand Final
Canterbury 11 • St George 9

1943 Grand Final
Newtown 34 • Norths 7

1944 Grand Final
Balmain 12 • Newtown 8

1945 Final
Easts 22 • Balmain 18

1946 Grand Final
Balmain 13 • St George 12

1947 Grand Final
Balmain 13 • Canterbury 9

1948 Grand Final
Wests 8 • Balmain 5

1949 Final
St George 19 • Souths 12

Team Changes

Manly-Warringah and Parramatta entered the League in 1947, taking the number of teams to 10.

Did You Know?

Ray Lindwall, one of Australia's greatest Test cricket fast bowlers, started his sporting career as a fullback at St George alongside his brother Jack.

Above: St George's first premiership-winning team, 1941

St George win their first title, 1941

It took the great St George club 20 years to win their first title. It was their young captain-coach Neville Smith who, at the age of 23, turned the club around. In 1941, Saints defeated the mighty Balmain side, 32–8, in the semi-final and then beat Easts 31–14 in the final to claim their first ever premiership.

St George were very unlucky not to win other titles in the 1940s – they lost the grand final in 1942 to Canterbury, and in 1946 and 1948 they lost to Balmain. In 1949, they beat Souths in the premiership final to claim their second title.

Having won two premierships in the 1940s, Saints would go on and dominate the 1950s and 1960s.

Balmain in the 1940s: 'The Benchmark Club'

In the 1940s, an era dominated by World War II, Balmain missed just one finals series, in 1940, when they finished fifth, just one point outside the top four.

After failing to advance past the semi-finals for three straight years, Balmain claimed an impressive title win in 1944. They defeated Newtown in a controversial final, 19–16, amid reports that Newtown let Balmain win, so that a second final could be played, drawing another big crowd and more money. Balmain then beat Newtown again in the grand final 12–8.

After losing the premiership decider to Easts in 1945, Balmain had to beat St George twice in the finals in 1946 to win another title. They then beat Canterbury twice in 1947 to take the premiership before losing the 1948 grand final to Wests.

Above: Balmain captain Tom Bourke (centre) leads Balmain out onto the field, 1947.

Above: Parramatta's first team, 1947.

Manly and Parramatta Enter the League, 1947

Manly-Warringah and Parramatta were both promoted to the 1st grade competition in 1947. Manly had been reasonably successful as part of the North Sydney junior competition and had requested to join the top grade in 1937 and 1944.

Parramatta too had tried to gain entry into the competition in previous years with no luck. They had a taste of the top grade with the Cumberland team in 1908 but had since competed as part of the Western Suburbs Junior League.

Above: Manly's first team, 1947.

1940s

Interstate Rugby League Resumes, 1945

The annual series between the two states continued until 1941, two years after the start of World War II, before being put on hold until 1945, the year the war ended. Both states were decimated by the war years, but NSW picked up where they left off, winning both games in 1945 and all three games in 1946. They then won the 1947 series 2 games to 1 with the fourth game drawn 13 all. They won 3–1 in 1948 and then all four games in 1949. Queensland would not win another interstate match until 1951.

Right: NSW's Kevin Hansen playing against Brisbane, 1947.

CLIVE CHURCHILL: 'THE LITTLE MASTER'

Clive Churchill has long been regarded as the greatest player Australian Rugby League has produced. He came to Souths in 1948 from Newcastle, and was selected for City, NSW and Australia. In 1950, he took over as captain of Australia and won the Ashes at home. He would go on to play 99 consecutive representative games up until 1955.

Churchill ended his Test career in 1956, having played 37 Tests, most as captain. He then became captain-coach of South Sydney in 1958 before playing a final year in Brisbane. He coached Queensland and Australia before returning to his beloved Souths, where he claimed another four premierships as coach in 1967, 1968, 1970 and 1971.

The Internationals, 1940s. 'The Return of Test Football'

The year after the War ended, England – now called Great Britain – returned to Australia for the first Ashes Test series since 1937–38. The Lions travelled to Australia aboard the warship *Invincible*, which also brought back many of the soldiers from Europe. Both teams were understrength, a whole generation of players having missed the chance to play Test football because of the War, but England proved too strong in this series.

In 1948, Australia played two Tests against New Zealand, with both sides winning a game each. On the night of the Second Test in Brisbane, the 1948–49 Kangaroos were selected to go to England and France. In a major snub, Australian captain coach Len Smith (a 1939 Rugby Union representative) was left out of the touring squad by the selectors. Smith retired from the game.

On tour, Australia lost all three Tests against England, although they managed a series win against the French.

In 1949, Australia travelled to New Zealand by seaplane and played a Two-Test series against the Kiwis. Each team won a Test, but Australia had improved greatly and the 1950s would be much more successful.

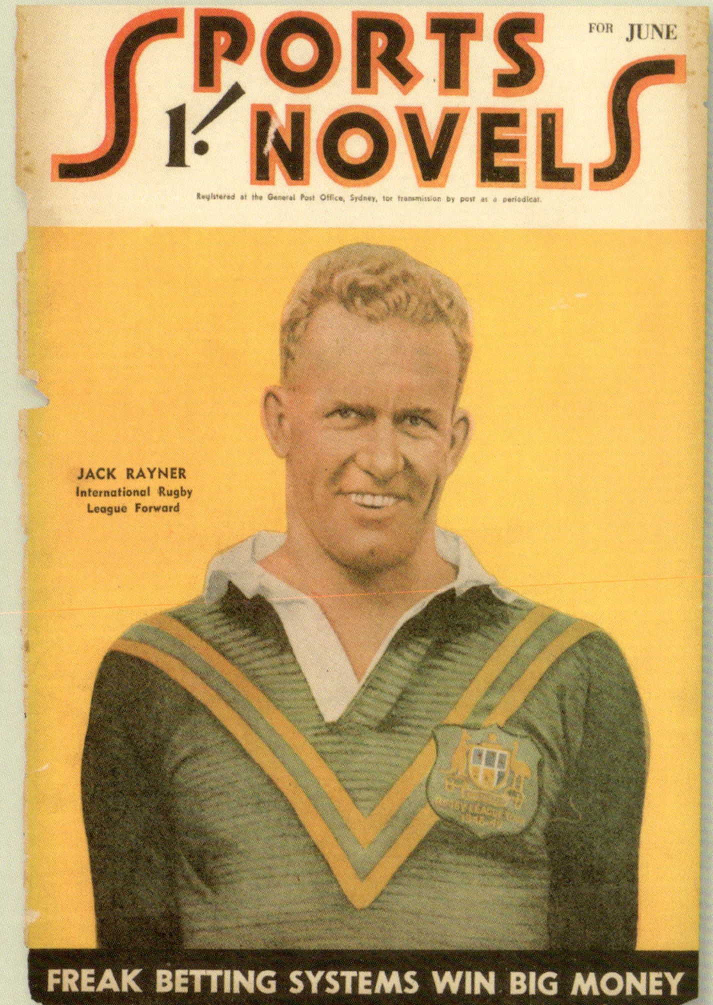

Above: 1948–49 Kangaroo, Jack Rayner.
Below: Captain Bill Tyquin leads Australia out for the Third Test at Bradford, 1948.

1950s

The Premiers

1950 Final
Souths 21 • Wests 15

1951 Grand Final
Souths 42 • Manly 14

1952 Final
Wests 22 • Souths 12

1953 Grand Final
Souths 31 • St George 12

1954 Grand Final
Souths 23 • Newtown 15

1955 Grand Final
Souths 12 • Newtown 11

1956 Grand Final
St George 18 • Balmain 12

1957 Grand Final
St George 31 • Manly 9

1958 Grand Final
St George 20 • Wests 9

1959 Grand Final
St George 20 • Manly 0

Did You Know?

In 1959, St George became the last club to go throughout a season undefeated. They were the fifth side to be undefeated in a season after Balmain (1915), Norths (1921), Souths (1925) and Easts (1936 and 1937).

The 'Mandatory' Grand Final, 1954

In 1954, the League made the decision to scrap the 'grand final challenge' system that had been in place since 1926, which meant that the Minor Premier would always play in the premiership decider. Instead, 1 v 2 and 3 v 4; the winner of the first match went into the grand final while the loser played the winning team of the second match for the right to go in the grand final.

This change came about due to a number of reasons. The League needed to have a set schedule so as to ensure they could book the venues they needed (the SCG had to be prepared for cricket).

Plus, the grand final had quickly become known as the ultimate club contest so why not have one every year!

Below: Action from the 1954 grand final between Souths and Newtown.

Glory, Glory to South Sydney! 1950–1955

South Sydney returned to the top of the Premiership in 1950 and over the next six seasons they won five titles. The only blip in the run was in 1952, when Wests won a controversial grand final 22–12. Many of Souths' best players, including Clive Churchill, had already left Sydney to sail for England with the 1952–53 Kangaroos.

Clive Churchill.

Interestingly, Churchill did not captain South Sydney. The Rabbitohs were captain-coached by Test forward Jack Rayner. Other great Souths players from this era include Bernie Purcell, Johnny Greaves, Ian Moir, Les Cowie and Greg Hawick.

Souths' 'Miracle of 1955'

South Sydney's memorable winning run in the 1955 premiership has been labelled 'the miracle of '55.'

After ten games, Souths were just one win ahead of last-placed Parramatta. They then won all of their remaining eight games to sneak into the finals. Their second-last win before the finals saw champion Clive Churchill kick the match-winning goal from the sideline after the fulltime siren had sounded, despite having broken his arm earlier in the game. It was wrapped up in a makeshift splint made of tape and the cardboard cover of an exercise book.

Souths then beat Manly and St George in the finals, before their stunning 12–11 victory over Newtown in the grand final.

Above: Souths' premiership-winning team, 1951.

KEN KEARNEY: 'THE KILLER'

Ken Kearney was a consummate professional in everything he did. This was a huge factor in his long and successful career as a player and coach in English club football, at St George and for Australia.

'Killer' Kearney started his career playing Rugby Union for Parramatta before enlisting with the Air Force in World War II. He switched codes and joined Leeds in England in 1948, where he starred as a hooker. Returning to Australia in 1952, he joined glamour club St George and brought to the club many of the successful English football traits, including the famous 'straight wall of defence'.

Kearney captain-coached St George in five of their 11 straight grand finals wins (he wasn't coach in 1956 and didn't play in the 1961 grand final because of injury). He also played 31 Tests for Australia, captaining the 1956–57 Kangaroos, before retiring as a player in 1961. He later coached Parramatta and Wests, and was Cronulla's foundation coach in 1967.

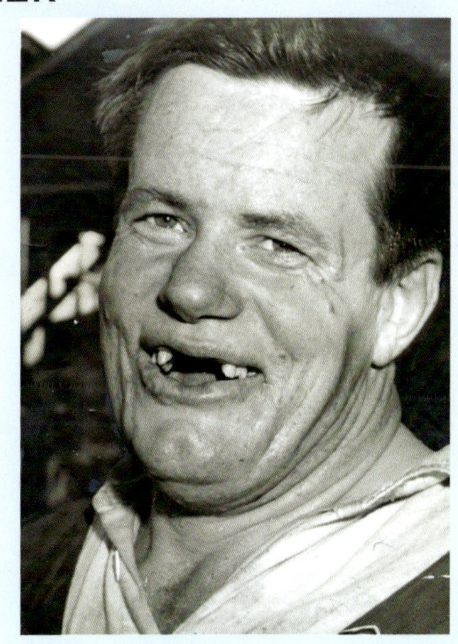

1950s

March of the Dragons: 1956–1966 (Part 1)

In 1956, St George claimed the minor premiership in the final round of competition, pipping Balmain by a solitary premiership point. Later that month, St George defeated Balmain 18–12 in the grand final in front of 61,987 fans at the SCG. Little did anyone know that it would be the start of the most dominant dynasty in Australian sport.

The following year, the Dragons toppled Manly in a lopsided final, 31–9. The 1958 decider against Wests was the first of several major clashes between the two sides during the Dragons' premiership reign, with this result going St George's way, 20–9.

The 1959 St George team were the last to go through a season undefeated, recording 17 wins and a draw from their 18 premiership games. They then beat Manly and Wests in the finals before comfortably winning the title with a brutal, 20–0 win over Manly.

Above: The St George team that was undefeated in 1959.

Above: France celebrate victory against Australia in the 1951 Test series.

Above: Ron Roberts scores the Ashes winning try, 1950.

Australia wins the Ashes, 1950

In 1950, Australia won their first Ashes Test series against Great Britain in thirty years. Led by the champion Clive Churchill and coached by former Test five-eighth Vic Hey, Australia took on Great Britain at the SCG in the deciding Third Test of the series after heavy rain turned the ground into a quagmire. In an excitingly hard match, Australia scored the only try to win 5–2. When St George winger Ron Roberts dived over in the corner, it gave the home team their first win in an Ashes series since 1920.

Here Come the French! 1951

After Australia's Test series win over France at the end of the 1937–38 Kangaroo tour, no Test matches were played until after the end of World War II in 1945. The game in France quickly blossomed once again, with France becoming one of the best sides in the world during the 1950s. Led by their enigmatic goal-kicking fullback, Puig Aubert, who was widely regarded as the French Clive Churchill, France played a wildly unpredictable brand of Rugby League intent on throwing the ball around rather than just defending.

France defeated Australia on their 1951 tour, and then repeated the feat in 1955. The French, known as *Le Chanticleer* (the Roosters) were *magnifique!*

The United States 'Tomahawks' in Australia, 1953

The United States of America sent a team of players to Australia in 1953, however their tour was not that successful despite some spirited performances from players with little experience and understanding of the game. The US 'Tomahawks' drew a lot of attention but were out of their depth playing Rugby League against the hardened Australians. They were entertaining, and at times competitive, but were well-beaten by NSW and Queensland teams and did not play a Test match because they just weren't good enough.

Team Mascots

The 1950s saw each team adopt an official mascot.

Balmain changed from the 'Watersiders' to the Tigers because of their black and orange strip.

Easts, known as the 'Tricolours' for their red, white and blue jerseys, adopted the Roosters following the success of France in the 1950s, (*Le Chanticleer*), who wore the same colours.

Souths were called the Rabbitohs after the rabbit sellers in Redfern where the club was based.

Newtown were affectionately called the Bluebags after stories of their jumpers being made of blue sugar bags. In the 1970s they became the Jets as they were located near Sydney airport.

Norths adopted the Bears in 1950 after their major club sponsor, Big Bear Supermarket.

Wests were the 'fruit pickers' initially after the farms in their area, prior to becoming the Magpies in 1928. They were the first club with an official mascot on their jersey.

St George claimed the Dragons from Saint George, the patron saint of England who 'slayed dragons'.

In the late 1970s, journalist Geoff Prenter suggested that Canterbury change to the Bulldogs after the club had been known as 'The Berries.'

Manly displayed a Sea Eagle on their jerseys, which is a bird native to their area, after being known as 'Seagulls' for many years.

Journalist Peter Frilingos suggested Parramatta adopt the 'Eels' mascot based on the local Aboriginal name for the area ('Burramatta' ... 'the place where the eels lie down').

1950s

The Inaugural World Cup, 1954

After much hard work by the French Rugby League, the first World Cup was staged there in 1954. The four major Rugby League nations – Great Britain, France, Australia and New Zealand – took part. The southern hemisphere teams were not successful that year and Great Britain defeated France in the final, 16–12.

1954 in England

Round 1 – lost 28–13 v Great Britain
Round 2 – won 34–15 v NZ
Round 3 – lost 15–5 v France

1957 World Cup in Australia

In 1957, Rugby League celebrated its 50th season in Australia and so the League hosted the second World Cup. Australia was captain-coached by Newtown centre Dick Poole and was undefeated in the three preliminary rounds. There was no need for a final, with Australia declared the winner.

Round 1 – won 25–5 v New Zealand
Round 2 – won 31–6 v Great Britain
Round 3 – won 26–9 v France

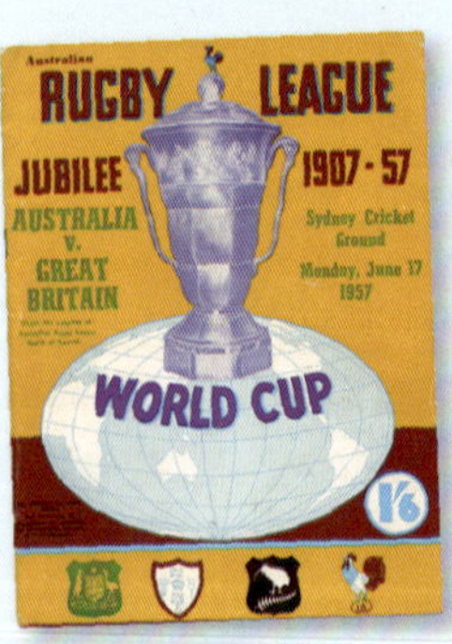

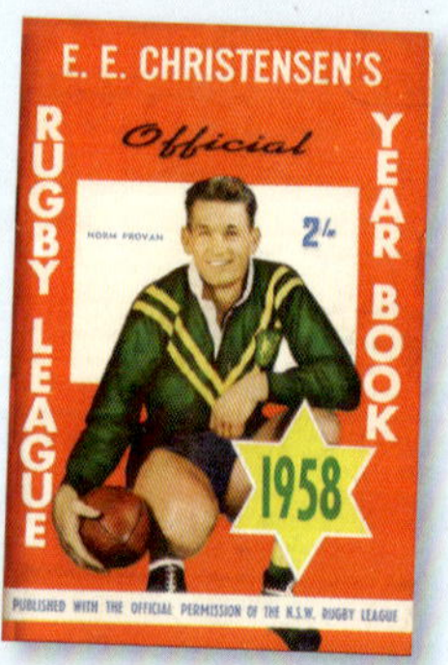

Did You Know?

Because there was no World Cup Final in 1957, Australia played a 'Rest of the World' team made of the best players from the other nations. Australia won that match too, 20–11.

Above: Australia's first World Cup team, 1954.

Rule Changes, 1950s

By the 1950s many rule changes had been trialled, some successfully, while others had failed. In the early years of the game, for example, if a player kicked a loose ball over the crossbar, they were awarded a field goal. Also, if you caught the ball on the full from a kick, you could take a shot at goal. Both of these rules were abolished before the war.

In the 1920s it was suggested that referees should feed scrums. This idea was short-lived but it led to halfbacks taking on the role permanently.

The current play the ball rule, allowing two players from each side to be in the ruck, was introduced in 1926 and remained in place until 1997.

Below: Keith Holman (Wests) and Noel Mulligan (St George) shake hands after a match.

The Internationals, 1950s

Winning the Ashes in England remained out of reach for three Kangaroo tours during the 1950s. In 1952–53, the Clive Churchill led Kangaroos were well-beaten in England and then lost the three Test series against France. In 1954, Australia again won the Ashes at home but winning a series in England remained incredibly hard to do.

In 1956–57, Ken Kearney captain-coached the Kangaroos, who were unlucky to lose in England (one Test was postponed because of bad fog!). They defeated France 3 Tests to nil, however, for the first time. The following year, Great Britain defended the Ashes in Australia, winning two Tests to one.

A goal attempt that hit the posts in Australia's 11–10 loss in the Second Test cost the 1959–60 Kangaroos the Ashes. Captain-coached by legendary Balmain fullback Keith Barnes, this squad narrowly defeated France and then played two matches in Italy on the way back to Australia.

Above: The 1959–60 Kangaroos squad that toured England, France and Italy.

REG GASNIER: 'PUFF, THE MAGIC DRAGON'

Nicknamed 'Puff the Magic Dragon,' Gasnier possessed lightning quick acceleration, a great step and swerve, good defence and anticipation. 'Gaz' was signed by St George at the age of 18 and made his 1st grade debut in 1959. That year, he was selected for NSW after just five games and made his Test debut for Australia against New Zealand.

In 1962, he was named captain of the Australian side, breaking Dave Brown's record as the youngest ever captain, aged 22 years and 28 days. In 1964, he was captain-coach of the Kangaroos. He won a premiership with the Dragons in every year of his career except for his last season, in 1967.

A series of injuries eventually led to his premature retirement at the age of 28, as captain-coach of the 1967–68 Kangaroos. In his brief time in the game, Gasnier was labelled the best centre in the game's history having scored over 100 tries for the Dragons.

1960s

The Premiers

1960 Grand Final
St George 31 • Easts 6

1961 Grand Final
St George 22 • Wests 0

1962 Grand Final
St George 9 • Wests 6

1963 Grand Final
St George 8 • Wests 3

1964 Grand Final
St George 11 • Balmain 6

1965 Grand Final
St George 12 • Souths 8

1966 Grand Final
St George 23 • Balmain 4

1967 Grand Final
Souths 12 • Canterbury 10

1968 Grand Final
Souths 13 • Manly 9

1969 Grand Final
Balmain 11 • Souths 2

Team Changes

Cronulla-Sutherland and Penrith entered the League in 1967.

Did You Know?

Cronulla were originally to wear brown and gold colours and be called 'the Lions'. The Penrith Panthers asked if they could use brown. Cronulla agreed and chose the black, white and blue of the Cronulla Surf Life Saving Club and were called the Sharks.

'The Gladiators', 1963

As the players walked off the field at the end of a controversial 1963 Grand Final, where St George won their eighth straight Premiership, opposing captains Norm Provan (St George) and Arthur Summons (Wests) were photographed in an embrace by photographer John O'Gready.

This photo became known as 'The Gladiators' and came to symbolise the sportsmanship and friendship in the game.

In 1982, a bronze statue based on this photo became the premiership trophy, which is still used today.

Above: Norm Provan and Arthur Summons recreate the famous 'Gladiators' photo from 1963, which became the basis for the NRL premiership trophy.

Above: The 1964 grand final between St George and Balmain as shown on TV.

Rugby League on TV, 1960s

Before the 1960s, footage of Rugby League games was shot on film and only shown in cinemas. In 1956, however, black and white television was launched in Australia and the following year the first game was shown on TV. By 1961, Rugby League was broadcast on TV into people's homes on a weekly basis.

As the years rolled on, the quality of the coverage improved. Former Test player Rex Mossop was the best-known commentator and was the outspoken host of a program called 'Controversy Corner' discussing 'pertinent League matters'.

The 1965 grand final: '78,056 at the SCG!'

In 1965, a young talented South Sydney side beat premiers St George in both premiership games. When the two teams met later than year in the grand final, a record crowd of 78,056 packed the SCG to see if Saints' run of premiership titles would end.

There were so many people trying to get into the match the SCG had to shut its gates two hours before kick-off. Thousands of fans climbed into the ground, sat on the grandstand roof or took vantage points looking into the ground from the Sydney Showground next door.

St George lead 5–4 at half-time but in the second half, Johnny King scored the winning try and Souths could not crack the Dragons' straight wall of defence. St George's Norm Provan retired after the game, having played in ten straight grand final wins, the last four as captain coach.

Right: St George captain-coach Norm Provan farewells Rugby League after the 1965 grand final. Provan won a record ten straight grand finals with Saints (1956–1965).

1960s

Above: St George captain-coach Ian Walsh is chaired from the field after the 1966 grand final.

The March of the Dragons, 1956–66 (Part 2)

The Dragons began the 1960s where they left off, winning grand final after grand final. After beating Easts in 1960, the Dragons beat Wests in three consecutive grand finals (1961–63).

The 1963 grand final was played in torrential rain and on a very muddy SCG pitch. The Dragons won a dour battle, 8–3, amid controversies over the performance of referee Darcy Lawler. The key moment came with the Dragons leading 5–3 when star winger Johnny King appeared to be tackled by Wests' Don Parish. King slipped out of the tackle while on the ground and raced away to score the winning try.

In 1965, a record SCG crowd of 78,056 witnessed St George win its tenth straight title over Souths, 12–8.

The Dragons beat Balmain in 1964 and 1966 but lost both finals matches in 1967 to Souths and Canterbury, ending their world record run of 11 straight premiership titles.

JOHN RAPER: 'THE PRINCE OF LOCKS'

John Raper is regarded as the greatest lock forward Australia has ever produced. He began his 1st grade career as a teenager at Newtown aged 18 before moving to St George in 1959. Raper became an integral member of the club's champion teams in the 1960s.

He quickly represented City, NSW and Australia in 1959. Arguably his greatest performance was in the Second Test of the 1963–64 Kangaroo Tour, when he was the best player in Australia's 50–12 win over Great Britain at Swinton. He later captained Australia in 1964, against South Africa and New Zealand, and on the 1967–68 Kangaroo Tour. In 1968, he was Australia's winning World Cup captain.

Raper finished his Sydney career as captain-coach of St George in 1969 but could not return the club to their premiership-winning ways. He moved to Newcastle in 1970, but his Test career was over. He later coached Cronulla for two seasons and Newtown in 1978 for half a season, before becoming a Test selector.

The Internationals, 1960s (Part 1)

1960 was a busy year for Test football. France travelled to Australia where they lost both Test series to Australia and New Zealand. Great Britain won the 1960 World Cup in England, beating Australia in the preliminary rounds.

The early 1960s was not a successful era for Australian Rugby League; the Kangaroos could only draw the series against the Kiwis in three tours across the Tasman (1961, 1965 and 1969) and when the British Lions toured Australia in 1962, they easily retained the Ashes.

1963 was another hectic year for Rugby League. Australia beat New Zealand 2–1 in a home Test series and then thrashed South Africa in two Tests. The Kangaroos ventured to England and France in the winter of 1963–64 with no real expectation of winning the Ashes. No Australian team had won the Ashes in England for more than 50 years, but how wrong the critics were.

Above: Arthur Summons.

Captain-coached by Arthur Summons, but led by St George's Ian Walsh in the Tests because Summons was injured, the Kangaroos won the First Test, 28–2. They then thrashed Great Britain in the 'Swinton Massacre' by a record score of 50 points to 12, to win the Ashes series.

Below: Australia's Dick Thornett scores a try the Second Test against Great Britain at Swinton in 1963. The Kangaroos won 50–12 to win the Ashes for the first time in England.

1960s

Australia in the World Cup

1960 in England

Round 1 – won 13–12 v France
Round 2 – won 21–15 v NZ
Round 3 – lost 10–3 to Great Britain

1968 World Cup in Australia

To mark the 60th anniversary of Rugby League in Australia, the home team again hosted the World Cup competition. Captained by John Raper and coached by Harry Bath, Australia were undefeated in the competition and won the final against France, 20–2.

1968 Results

Round 1 – won 25–10 v Great Britain
Round 2 – won 31–12 v New Zealand
Round 3 – won 37–4 v France
Final – won 20–2 v France

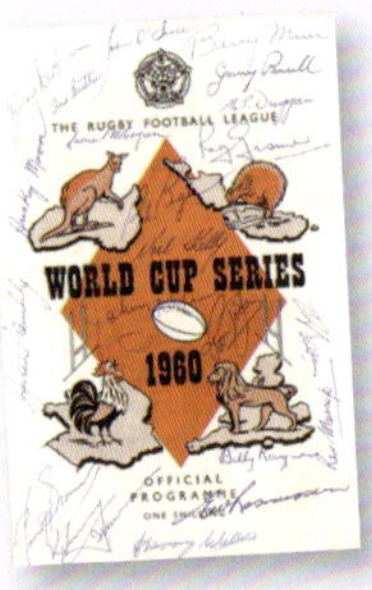

Did You Know?

In 1967, the game went from the same unlimited tackle rule as Rugby Union, to a limited tackle rule. The new rule limited a team's possession to just four tackles before a scrum was set and the ball was contested again.

Many fans saw this rule as a way to make the game even more exciting while others believed it was done to end St George's dominance in the game. Whatever the reason, the Dragons did not win a grand final for another ten years!

The Rabbitohs Reign Supreme, 1967–68

After the end of St George's 11-season premiership dominance, a new era began with South Sydney. The Rabbitohs won back-to-back titles in 1967 and 1968 and by the end of the decade their star-studded team – John Sattler, Ron Coote, Bob McCarthy, Denis Pittard, Eric Simms, Mike Cleary – was at their peak.

Souths' fast paced style and ability to keep the ball alive saw them flourish under the limited tackle rule. In 1967, they defeated Canterbury 12–10, largely because of an intercept try to Bob McCarthy and the goal-kicking of Eric Simms. The following year Souths beat Manly, 13–9, in a close match.

Below: Balmain v Souths, Grand Final 1969.

Above: Souths 1967 Grand Final team.

Balmain Upsets Souths in the 1969 Grand Final

In 1969, the all-conquering Souths team took on a depleted Balmain side to try and win their third straight grand final. Souths had broken all records in 1969 and were short-priced favourites against a Tigers team missing Arthur Beetson, who was suspended for fighting, and other star players who were injured.

Balmain intentionally slowed the play down, upsetting the fast-paced Souths attack. In the second half, and leading 6–0, the Tigers players went down injured, stopping the play (as was the rule at the time). Balmain went on to win the match 11–2 in what is regarded as the greatest upset in the game's history.

Scanlen's Football Cards

In 1963, Scanlen's bubble gum company started a craze when they included pictures of Rugby League stars in packs of bubble gum. By the end of the decade, children were buying the 20c packs in their thousands and collecting the cards (and eating the bubble gum!).

In 1994, Dynamic got the card-collecting industry going again and then, in 2000, Select took over and have continued the tradition of producing brilliant sets of player cards and keeping the collecting craze alive.

1960s

The Internationals, 1960s (Part 2): Australia wins the Ashes in England

In 1966, Great Britain came to Australia to try and recapture the Ashes. Ian Walsh was captain-coach but selectors would not give him the team he wanted. In the deciding Third Test, Walsh finally got what he wanted – Arthur Beetson! Australia won the match, 19–14 at the SCG, with Beetson proving to be the match-winner.

The 1967–68 Kangaroo Tour to England and France was marred by the injury to captain-coach Reg Gasnier and ill-discipline from some of the team. With their backs against the wall, the John Raper-led Australians retained the Ashes with an 11–3 win on a frozen Swinton ground. Unfortunately, the poor attitude returned in France and Australia lost the series there.

Australia easily won the 1968 World Cup before rounding out the decade with another tied series with New Zealand in 1969.

Below: The 1967–68 Ashes-winning Kangaroos, captain-coached by the great Reg Gasnier.

Graeme Langlands: 'Chang-a-lang'

Graeme Langlands is widely regarded as one of the most talented backs to ever play the game. Over his career he played at centre, wing and most notably, at fullback. He was first spotted playing for NSW Country where he helped them win a rare match against City in 1962, earning him selection for NSW that year. Signed by St George, he made his Test debut the following season.

Langlands won four straight premierships with the Dragons (1963–66) but after many of the club's great players retired he took over as captain-coach in the 1970s. During this period, he was also captain-coach of Australia, leading the Kangaroos to Ashes success in 1973 and 1974, as well as the 1972 and 1975 World Cup campaigns. Langlands was a match-winner and a great competitor.

A stray painkilling injection before the 1975 grand final to treat a groin injury contributed to what was the worst match of his career, however, as it numbed his right leg and he could not stop the Roosters from winning 38–0. It was made even more memorable by the bright white boots he wore that day (all players wore black boots at the time). 'Chang' ended his career the following season, the greatest point scorer in Dragon history, finishing with 1,554 points.

Dennis Tutty: 'Man of Honour'

In 1960, the residential rule was replaced by a 'transfer' rule, which meant clubs had full control over their players' careers if they refused to let them transfer to other clubs. In 1967, Balmain Test lock Dennis Tutty asked for a release from the club to join Penrith, but they refused. Tutty continued asking Balmain, and even the League, to release him but was denied every time.

Tutty stopped playing as a protest midway through 1968, missing the entire 1969 season and Balmain's grand final win. The club still would not release him so Tutty took the matter to the Equity Court which ruled that Balmain's refusal of his transfer requests were a 'restraint of trade'.

The League appealed the decision to the High Court. In 1971, the court upheld the Equity Court's decision, thereby ending the code's unfair transfer system. Tutty had won the right to play for any club he wanted to and this was the beginning of the 'club contract' system players sign today.

Below: Balmain players Dennis Tutty and Peter Jones have their case heard in the NSW Equity Court, 1969.

1970s

The Premiers

1970 Grand Final
Souths 23 • Manly 12

1971 Grand Final
Souths 16 • St George 10

1972 Grand Final
Manly 19 • Easts 14

1973 Grand Final
Manly 10 • Cronulla 7

1974 Grand Final
Easts 19 • Canterbury 4

1975 Grand Final
Easts 38 • St George 0

1976 Grand Final
Manly 13 • Parramatta 10

1977 Grand Final
St George 9 • Parramatta 9

Grand Final Replay
St George 22 • Parramatta 0

1978 Grand Final
Manly 11 • Cronulla 11

Grand Final Replay
Manly 16 • Cronulla 0

1979 Grand Final
St George 17 • Canterbury 13

Did You Know?

The 1977 and 1978 grand finals both ended in a draw, forcing the games to be played again. In both replays, the winning teams kept their opponents scoreless!

Above: Australia's World Cup squad, 1970.
Below: John O'Neill after the 1970 World Cup final.

The 1970 World Cup Final: 'The Battle of Leeds'

The end of the 1970 season found Australian Rugby League at an all-time low. Having lost the Ashes to Great Britain that year, the Kangaroos had to travel to England at the end of the year to play in a World Cup. Potential captains Graeme Langlands (broken hand) and John Sattler (broken jaw) were ruled out of the squad, leaving Souths lock Ron Coote to be named captain.

An understrength Australian team barely made the final against the home side at Leeds and were given no chance of winning. Great Britain threw everything at the Kangaroos – punching, kicking, fighting – but Australia played good football and won a famous victory, 12–8.

John Sattler's Courage, 1970

The 1970 grand final has been synonymous for one act of courage. Ten minutes into the game, Souths' Test forward and captain John Sattler broke his jaw after a high, off-the-ball incident involving a Manly forward.

Rather than leave the field, 'Satts' played on in agony without letting his opponents and many of his teammates know that he was seriously injured. Continuing to tackle and run the ball up with his jaw broken in two places, he stayed on the field to guide his champion team to a 23–12 win.

Right: John Sattler (with headband) breaks his jaw.

JACK GIBSON: 'SUPERCOACH'

Jack Gibson was a good player in his 12 seasons in 1st grade, but he was a champion coach. In 1967, in his first season as coach, he took an Easts team that had not won a match in 1966 to the finals. And he did it again in 1968!

Gibson then moved to the Dragons in 1970, taking them to the grand final against Souths the following year. He joined Newtown in 1973 and the struggling club improved so much it won the Club Championship.

Gibson returned to Easts in 1974, and won two premierships there. Gibson opted for light-weight but mobile forwards with high work-rates rather than star players. He didn't tolerate bad behaviour or foul play and brought many professional innovations to our game from American football. His players were fitter, keener and sharper!

Although his time at Souths (1978–79) and Cronulla (1986–87) was not as successful, the supercoach's greatest success was in winning three straight grand finals with Parramatta Eels in 1981, '82 and '83. In 2008, the year he died, Gibson was named the best coach in the history of Rugby League.

1970s

Above: Fighting breaks out in the 1973 grand final between Manly and Cronulla.

The Manly Sea Eagles: 'Champions of the 1970s'

The Manly-Warringah Sea Eagles dominated the 1970s, missing the finals only once (1979) and winning four premiership titles (1972–73, 1976 and 1978). Manly was known as 'the bridesmaids' of the League, having been beaten in five premiership deciders before breaking through for their first grand final win in 1972.

The big spending Sea Eagles bought many new players to the club, including Englishman Mal Reilly and Souths' trio Bob Moses, John O'Neill and Ray Branighan, and were too good for Easts in the 1972 grand final, winning 19–14. The following year they toppled Cronulla in the grand final, 10–7, in the most violent match of modern times. Bob Fulton proved the difference between the two teams, scoring both of Manly's tries.

Manly became the team every club wanted to beat, but after bowing out of the finals campaigns early in 1974 and 1975, the Bob Fulton-led Sea Eagles bounced back to beat a brave Parramatta team, 13–10 in the 1976 grand final.

In 1978, Manly won over a legion of new fans with an arduous finals campaign where they had to play five games in 16 days to win the premiership title. The grand final against Cronulla finished in an 11–all draw but three days later, inspired by fullback Graham Eadie, Manly won 16–0.

BOB FULTON: 'BOZO WAS NO CLOWN'

English-born, Wollongong-bred Bob Fulton was still a teenager when he was signed by Manly in 1966. With his blonde hair, athletic physique and undeniable will to win, 'Bozo' as his teammates called him, quickly became a crowd favourite. He made his debut for Australia in the 1968 World Cup but also had to complete his National Service duties with the Australian Army during the Vietnam war. He served as a strength, fitness and conditioning officer.

Fulton was an important part of Manly's success in the 1970s but quit the club after the 1976 grand final to sign with Easts. In 1978 he had the honour of captaining Australia against New Zealand before leading the Kangaroos to England and France.

Fulton started his coaching career at Easts but returned to Manly as coach in 1983. Four years later he coached the Sea Eagles to grand final success, and repeated the feat in 1996. In between these two premiership titles, he coached Australia to Ashes victory in 1990, 1992 and 1994, as well as to World Cup success in 1992 and 1995.

Above: The Ashes-winning 1973 Kangaroos, captain-coached by Graeme Langlands.
Below: Australian captain-coach Graeme Langlands accepts the Ashes trophy after the 1974 Test series.

The Internationals, 1970s (Part 1): Winning back the Ashes!

In 1970 Great Britain came to Australia and shocked the home-team by winning the 3-Test series. After being thrashed in the First Test in Brisbane, 37–15, the British fought back to win the next two Tests with superior ball-play. However, this would be the last time Great Britain won the Ashes to date (48 years!).

Australia then returned the favour in 1973, losing the First Test at Wembley Stadium, 21–12, before winning the next two Tests to reclaim the Ashes. Australia used four different captains on the 1973 Kangaroo Tour – Graeme Langlands, Bob McCarthy, Tom Raudonikis and Arthur Beetson.

Great Britain returned to Australia in 1974, but they were an older and slower team. St George fullback Graeme Langlands was named captain-coach, but selectors sacked him as a player after Australia's poor form in winning the First Test in Brisbane. Australia then lost the Second Test, and with the Ashes at stake, Langlands was reinstated and led the Kangaroos to a 22–18 victory.

1970s

Australia in the World Cup

1970 in England

Round 1 – won 47–11 v NZ
Round 2 – lost 11–4 v Great Britain
Round 3 – lost 17–15 v France
Final – won 12–7 v Great Britain

1972 in France

Round 1 – lost 27–21 v Great Britain
Round 2 – won 9–5 v NZ
Round 3 – won 31–9 v France
Final – drew 10 all v Great Britain*

* Great Britain declared winners because they defeated Australia earlier in the competition.

1975 in all countries

Round 1 – won 36–8 v New Zealand
Round 2 – won 30–13 v Wales
Round 3 – won 26–6 v France
Round 4 – drew 10 all v England
Round 5 – won 24–8 v NZ
Round 6 – won 18–6 v Wales
Round 7 – won 41–2 v France
Round 8 – lost 16–3 v England *

* Australia declared winners without playing a final

1977 in Australia and NZ

Round 1 – won 27–12 v New Zealand
Round 2 – won 21–9 v France
Round 3 – won 19–5 v Great Britain
Final – won 13–12 v Great Britain

Did You Know?

In the 1972 World Cup final in France, Australian captain-coach Graeme Langlands was denied a spectacular diving try fielding a high kick because the referee thought he was off-side.

Above: Queensland's Greg Veivers takes on NSW in 1977.

The Death of Interstate Football in the 1970s

Interstate football games between NSW and Queensland had continued into the 1970s despite regularly lopsided results in the Blues' favour. By the early 1970s, however, crowd figures started to drop.

At this time, whether a club was in NSW or Queensland determined which state the player played for. Part of the problem was that wealthy Sydney clubs used their money and profile to attract Queensland's best players south of the border. These players were then selected for NSW to play against their home state.

Queensland did not win a series in the 1970s and the interstate series was in desperate need of a shakeup. By the end of the decade, plans were underway to have a game between Queensland-born and NSW-born players, and State of Origin was born in 1980.

The Roosters of 1974–75: 'The Greatest Team Ever?'

The Eastern Suburbs teams of the mid 1970s set near-unbeatable benchmarks under the coaching of Jack Gibson. In the 1974 and 1975 seasons, they won 43 of their 50 games and captured premierships in both seasons. The Roosters defeated Canterbury in the 1974 grand final with a team that contained champion players such as Arthur Beetson, John Brass, Ron Coote, Russell Fairfax, Mark Harris, Johnny Mayes, John Peard and Elwyn Walters.

In the 1975 grand final, the Roosters thrashed St George by a record 38 points to 0. This is the famous match where injured Dragons captain Graeme Langlands wore white boots into the game and his every mistake was highlighted by his unusual footwear (today, every player wears coloured shoes!). Easts ran in eight tries against a tired St George team in what is arguably the greatest grand final attacking display ever seen at the SCG.

Above: Western Division wins the Amco Cup, 1974.
Below: Roosters players on their lap of honour, 1975.

The Pre-Season and Mid-Week Cups

In 1962, a preseason competition made up of three rounds of trial games and finals started. This ran prior to the start of the real competition until 1981 and was revived in the early 1990s. The most popular competition was the midweek AMCO Cup, which started in 1974. Teams from around the country competed in Wednesday night matches made up of four, twenty-minute quarters, which was ideal for TV. The competition's first winners were unheralded NSW Country team Western Division. The competition ran until 1988 when it was felt it was too hard for players to back up on the weekend.

1970s

The First Grand Final Draw: St George v Parramatta, 1977

In 1977, the game produced only its second ever drawn premiership decider after the 4–all tie between Souths and Newtown in 1910.

Late in the 1977 grand final, St George lead 9–6 when Parramatta's Ed Sulkowicz scored out wide to level the scores. Champion goal-kicking Test centre Mick Cronin lined up the conversion to win the game for the Eels but the kick missed.

With no further score after two ten-minute periods of extra-time, the grand final was replayed the following week. The young Dragons team came out firing and ran away with the game, winning 22–0. Parramatta would have to wait four more years for another chance at winning a

Above: Ray Price tackled by Rod Reddy in the 1977 grand final draw.

ARTHUR BEETSON: 'BIG ARTY'

Arthur Beetson was born in Roma, in central Queensland, and started his career as a winger. Signing with Redcliffe as an 18-year-old centre, he moved into the second row and came to Sydney to play with Balmain in 1966. He represented City, NSW and Australia in his first season but was criticised in the press for being unfit and a labelled a 'lazy' trainer.

Beetson missed Balmain's grand Final victory in 1969 due to suspension and left the club for Easts at the end of 1970 seeking a new start. At the Roosters, he developed into the best ball-playing forward in the world with an uncanny ability to slip a pass to a supporting player despite seemingly being tackled. In 1973, he became the first Indigenous sportsman to be named captain of an Australian team when he led the Kangaroos to victory against France.

Beetson took over as Easts captain in 1974, starting a wonderful partnership with coach Jack Gibson which saw them win premierships in consecutive years (1974–75).

In 1977, Beetson was Test captain but was controversially overlooked for Australia's World Cup team against New Zealand. He was reinstated by the League but he chose not to play in the match on principle. He later spent two seasons at Parramatta and played a major role in the birth of State of Origin in 1980 when he captained Queensland in the first game, which they won, 20–10.

Above: Exciting centre Steve Rogers scoring a try against Great Britain in 1979.

Below: Mick Cronin playing for Australia in 1979.

The Internationals, 1970s (Part 2): Australia unbeatable!

In the 1970s, no less than four World Cup competitions were held. The expanded 'World Series' competition in 1975 saw Great Britain compete as separate England and Wales teams. Not only did this weaken the competition, but the Australian game had also improved by leaps and bounds because of our superior club football.

On the 1978 Kangaroo Tour, Australia retained the Ashes but not before being given a scare with a loss in the Second Test of the series. The Kangaroos lost both Tests in France because the local referees caned Australia in the penalties. After this tour, neutral referees were used in Test matches.

In 1979, Great Britain came to Australia looking to win back the Ashes. The Kangaroos were too fast, too fit and too strong and became the first team to win an Ashes series three Tests to nil.

1980s

The Premiers

1980 Grand Final
Canterbury 18 • Easts 4

1981 Grand Final
Parramatta 20 • Newtown 11

1982 Grand Final
Parramatta 21 • Manly 8

1983 Grand Final
Parramatta 18 • Manly 6

1984 Grand Final
Canterbury 6 • Parramatta 4

1985 Grand Final
Canterbury 7 • St George 6

1986 Grand Final
Parramatta 4 • Canterbury 2

1987 Grand Final
Manly 18 • Canberra 8

1988 Grand Final
Canterbury 24 • Balmain 12

1989 Grand Final
Canberra 19 • Balmain 14*
* after 20 mins extra time

Team Changes
Canberra entered in 1982
Illawarra entered in 1982
Newtown left after 1983 season
Brisbane entered in 1988
Gold Coast entered in 1988
Newcastle entered in 1988

Did You Know?

The 1989 Grand Final was the first premiership decider since mandatory grand finals began in 1954 to be won at the end of extra time.

Above: Bob O'Reilly and Steve Edge hold the J.J.Giltinan Shield after Parramatta's success in the 1981 grand final.

Here Come the Eels! 1981–83

Entering the League in 1947, Parramatta struggled for the best part of three decades and finished last on 12 occasions. After grand final losses in 1976 and 1977, 'supercoach' Jack Gibson took over the Eels in 1981 and Parramatta reached the grand final against Newtown.

Parramatta won their first premiership title by defeating Newtown 20–11. That night, fans went to the Eels' home ground, Cumberland Oval, and burnt down the old grandstand!

The Eels then defeated Manly in consecutive grand finals in 1982 and 1983 to make it a hat-trick of premierships. Champion players such as captain Steve Edge, Mick Cronin, Ray Price, Brett Kenny, Peter Sterling, Steve Ella, Eric Grothe, Paul Taylor and Peter Wynn wore the blue and gold jersey with pride.

Newtown Gone, but Wests Fight Back!

By 1983, several clubs were in financially desperate situations. Newtown, suffering from a $1.5 million debt and struggling to draw crowds, became the first team to be axed from the competition since University in 1938. The plan was to give the Jets a year to regroup and have them return at Campbelltown in 1985. This did not eventuate.

Wests too were also axed in 1983, but after much fund raising and legal action, they won the right to be reinstated to the League. Plans for Newtown's return were scrapped and the Campbelltown junior league was taken over by the Magpies.

Below: Parramatta's 1983 grand final winning team. Back row: Geoff Bugden, Peter Wynn, Paul Mares, Eric Grothe, Stan Jurd. Second row: Mick Souter (trainer), David Liddiard, Steve Sharp, Ray Price, Mick Cronin, Brett Kenny, Steve Ella, Alf Richards (trainer). Front row: Denis Fitzgerald (Secretary), Paul Taylor, Jack Gibson (coach), Steve Edge (captain), Ron Massey (assistant coach), Peter Sterling, Arthur Drew (Club Chairman).

The Game Changes in the 1980s

In the wake of the violent play of the 1970s, the 1980s saw many changes to the game. Harsh penalties for illegal play were handed down by the League Judiciary, which had a tremendous effect in cleaning up the game. The message was clear – foul play would no longer be tolerated.

Scrums had also become an ugly blight on the game. After the collapse of a scrum left Penrith forward John Farragher a quadriplegic in 1978, the League vowed to clean up scrums.

Two important rule changes helped promote attacking football. In 1982, the League declared that goal kicks could no longer be taken after a scrum penalty was awarded. Also, the value of a try was increased from three points to four points in 1983 to entice teams to try and score more tries.

At the end of the decade, a 'salary cap' was introduced to stop clubs from going broke chasing good players and to essentially 'even out' the competition. The salary cap is still in place today.

1980s

The Birth of State of Origin, 1980

NSW and Queensland officials finally agreed to conduct a 'State of Origin' match at the end of the 1980 series after the stronger Blues team had won the first two matches. There was little interest in the game in Sydney – it wasn't even shown live on TV – but the Queensland fans cheered their hometown players, many of whom were wearing the Maroons jersey for the first time.

Inspired by Queensland captain Arthur Beetson, and playing budding champions Wally Lewis and Mal Meninga, the Maroons won the match before a cheering Brisbane crowd, 20 points to 10. State of Origin was here to stay!

State of Origin in the early 1980s was dominated by Queensland which won 8 of the first 11 games and the first three series (1982–84) in a row. It wasn't until 1985 that NSW finally won its first Origin series.

Above: Canterbury captain George Peponis chaired by his players after the 1980 grand final.
Below: Queensland's Wally Lewis and Allan Langer.

Canterbury: 'From Entertainers to Dogs of War!'

In the 1970s and early 1980s, Canterbury were known as 'The Entertainers' for their amazing attacking style of football. Coached by Ted Glossop, the Bulldogs defeated Easts in the 1980 grand final, with winger Steve Gearin scoring a spectacular try when he caught a high kick on the full.

But Rugby League was becoming more focused on defence and the Bulldogs were not as successful. In 1984, the club brought in Warren Ryan, who had a reputation for turning teams into defensively strong outfits, as coach.

Ryan turned the Bulldogs from 'The Entertainers' into the 'Dogs of War', a team best known for ruthless defence. Canterbury won back-to-back grand finals in 1984 and 1985 but were pipped, 4–2, in the 1986 grand final by Parramatta. After a poor year in 1987 where the Bulldogs failed to make the finals, Ryan was replaced by rookie coach Phil Gould in 1988. Ryan went to Balmain and steered the Tigers to the grand final – only to be beaten 24–12 by a Bulldogs team that had rediscovered their attacking flair under the guidance of 'Gus' Gould.

The Internationals, 1980s: 'Trans-Tasman Test Rivalry Reignited'

Australia defeated Great Britain in four series during the 1980s and thrashed the French touring team in 1981. What the Kangaroos desperately needed was some competition!

After touring New Zealand and winning easily there in 1980, the world champion Australian team played a two-Test series against the Kiwis in 1983. The Kangaroos won the Test in New Zealand, 18–4, to take their winning streak to 18 matches. No-one expected the Kiwis to beat Australia in Brisbane, but they did just that, winning 19–12. Coached by Arthur Beetson and captained by Wally Lewis, Australia took New Zealand too lightly and lost the game.

The same thing happened in 1985 and 1987. The Kangaroos went to New Zealand in 1985 and won the first two Tests easily. The Kiwis then won the Third Test 18–0 after the Kangaroos started arguing with each other on tour and didn't support the coach.

In 1986, Australia returned from England and France undefeated but lost the one-off Test against New Zealand in 1987 by 13 points to 6. They had taken the Kiwis for granted, and instead of concentrating on the game, some players argued with the referee – and lost!

Australia finished the decade by restating their superiority over the Kiwis, winning the 1989 Trans-Tasman Test series, 3–nil.

Below left: Australian captain Max Krilich playing against New Zealand in 1982.

Below right: Australian captain Wally Lewis playing against Great Britain in 1986.

1980s

Australia in the World Cup

1985–88, in all countries

Game 1 – lost 18–0 v New Zealand
Game 2 – won 32–12 v New Zealand
Game 3 – won 62–12 v Papua New Guinea
Game 4 – won 24–15 v Great Britain
Game 5 – won 52–0 v France
Game 6 – lost 26–12 v Great Britain
Game 7 – won 70–8 v Papua New Guinea
Game 8 – won via forfeit v France
Final – won 25–12 v New Zealand

Wayne Pearce.

Did You Know?

The World Cup competition changed in the 1980s. Instead of a dedicated series played over a few weeks, it was decided that the final Test match of each series would count as a World Cup fixture.

This system was played over three years and saw France forfeit three games due to code's financial difficulties there.

On the upside, it was the first World Cup to include Papua New Guinea, which produced a huge upset when they beat New Zealand, 24–22, in their only win of the World Cup.

Above: Parramatta wins the first Winfield Cup in 1982.

The Winfield Cup, 1982–1995

In 1982, Rugby League secured a lucrative sponsorship deal with cigarette company Winfield. This also saw the birth of the Winfield Cup trophy, a bronze cast of the 'Gladiators' photograph of Norm Provan and Arthur Summons caked in mud after the 1963 Grand Final.

The Winfield Cup went from strength to strength, coinciding with the inclusion of two new clubs from outside the Sydney area, Canberra and Illawarra.

Winfield's association ended after the 1995 season when the Australian Government banned cigarette sponsorship in sport.

Farewell to the SCG, 1987

Rugby League and the Sydney Cricket Ground have a long history starting in 1911 when the first game at the venue resulted in NSW's defeat of New Zealand, 35–10, in front of 48,200 fans.

The SCG was regularly used in the NSWRL competition in conjunction with the nearby Sydney Sports Ground, up until 1983. The Sports Ground and the SCG no.2 oval were both demolished in late 1986 for the construction of the Sydney Football Stadium, which was first used in 1988.

The 1987 Grand Final between Manly and Canberra was the last to be played at the SCG. Some Rugby League games have been played at the ground since, including a State of Origin game in 1997 and the Centenary Test between Australia and New Zealand in 2008.

Above right: Laurie Daley.
Above left: Fans sleep outside the SCG, 1974.
Below: Wests Tigers v St George Illawarra at the SCG, 2011.

The 1989 Grand Final: 'The Greatest Ever?'

The 1989 Grand Final between Balmain and Canberra has long been regarded as the greatest grand final ever played. The Tigers had lost the 1988 grand final to Canterbury and went into this match as firm favourites against a young Canberra Raiders outfit which barely snuck into the finals. The game was fast, exciting and went from end to end. Balmain lead 14–2 at the break, but Canberra fought back to level the scores 14–all at fulltime. Extra time saw Chris O'Sullivan knock over a field goal before Raiders' replacement Steve Jackson scored a determined try to seal the game 19–14, giving Canberra their first ever premiership.

1980s

Rugby League Expansion: The Broncos, the Knights and the Seagulls

In 1988, the 80th anniversary of Rugby League in Australia, the League included three new teams in the competition. The success of Canberra and Illawarra saw the League look beyond Sydney in order to grow the game further.

Newcastle had been in the League back in 1908 and 1909 before exiting to form their own competition north of Sydney. The Newcastle Knights had many players to choose from and were welcomed back with open arms.

Brisbane was also a natural inclusion to the expanding competition. The League allowed a consortium of businessmen to privately own the Brisbane franchise, which were called the Broncos. The Brisbane Broncos resented the League's control of the game from Sydney, a situation which would ultimately lead to the Super League split.

So that the Broncos would not have all of Queensland to choose from, the League allowed a team from the Gold Coast-Tweed Heads area to also enter the League. This privately-owned Seagulls club did not have the money to compete with Brisbane and struggled for success for much of the next decade.

WALLY LEWIS: 'THE KING'

Wally Lewis is regarded as the greatest five-eighth in the history of the game. He was also one of the most divisive personalities due to his passionate displays for his beloved Queensland, which at one stage, saw him being booed by fans in Sydney when he captained Australia.

Lewis represented the Australian Rugby Union schoolboy's side in 1977 but switched codes the following year, playing for Brisbane Valleys and Wynnum-Manly in the Brisbane competition. He was denied the chance to play for a Sydney club by the Queensland Rugby League in 1986 because he was such a drawcard. The introduction of the Broncos in 1988 finally allowed Sydney fans to see just how good a player Lewis was week to week.

Lewis made his state debut at age 19, and played lock in the first ever Origin match in 1980. He played in every Origin game from 1980 until an injury saw him miss Game 1 of the 1988 series. He made his Test debut in 1981 and was made captain in 1984. A broken arm in 1989 effectively ended his rep career and he was cut by the Broncos at the end of the season. He retired as captain-coach of the Gold Coast Club in 1992 and coached Queensland, in 1993–94, but lost both series. Lewis later became a sports newsreader and commentator in Brisbane.

The 1982 and 1986 Kangaroos: 'Unbeatables'

The 1982 Kangaroos that toured England and France were named 'The Invincibles' when they became the first Australian team not to lose a game on tour. Captained by Manly's Max Krilich, Australia won 22 games, including three Tests against Great Britain, an International against Wales and two Tests against France.

Four years later, the 1986 Kangaroos side repeated the feat and were undefeated in England and France, earning the name 'The Unbeatables'. Captained by the great Wally Lewis, the 1986 Kangaroos were a vastly stronger attacking team than their 1982 teammates.

Great Britain came to Australia in 1984 and 1988 to play for the Ashes, but they just weren't good enough. Wally Lewis captained Australia to victory in both series.

Above: 1986 Kangaroos jersey.
Below: The 1982 Kangaroos, which became the first Australian touring team to return from England and France unbeaten.

1990s

The Premiers

1990 Grand Final
Canberra 18 • Penrith 14

1991 Grand Final
Penrith 19 • Canberra 12

1992 Grand Final
Brisbane 28 • St George 8

1993 Grand Final
Brisbane 14 • St George 6

1994 Grand Final
Canberra 36 • Canterbury 12

1995 Grand Final
Sydney Bulldogs 17 • Manly 4

1996 Grand Final
Manly 20 • St George 8

1997 ARL Grand Final
Newcastle 22 • Manly 16

1997 Super League Grand Final
Brisbane 26 • Cronulla 8

1998 Grand Final
Brisbane 38 • Canterbury 12

1999 Grand Final
Melbourne 20 • St George-Illawarra 18

Did You Know?

In September 1997, there were suggestions that Super League Premiers Brisbane would play ARL champions Newcastle in a Superbowl type match to determine which team was the best in Australia. Unfortunately, this did not happen.

Above: Royce Simmons, 1991.

Penrith Panthers: 'Bound for Glory' 1991

The Penrith Panthers entered the competition in 1967 and had struggled for both success and credibility for almost two decades before making the finals for the first time in 1985 under the coaching of former player Tim Sheens. In 1990, under new coach Phil Gould, Penrith made their first grand final but fell agonisingly short against a star-studded Canberra team, 18–14.

In 1991, Penrith had five internationals in their team – Royce Simmons, Greg Alexander, Brad Fittler, Mark Geyer and John Cartwright (the last four all local juniors) – and were minor premiers. In the grand final against the Raiders, veteran hooker Royce Simmons scored two tries in his last game to help the Panthers to win their first title, 19–12, in the grand final.

The Brisbane Broncos: 'Back to Back Success', 1992–93

The Brisbane Broncos entered the League in 1988 with a State of Origin strength team and were expected to win titles almost immediately. It was not until 1992, however, that coach Wayne Bennett was able to balance the club's obligations to 'rep' football and club success.

In 1992, the Broncos fielded a brilliant team captained by halfback Allan Langer which beat St George, 28–8, in the grand final. The following year, the Broncos came from fifth on the ladder to deny St George again in the grand final, winning 14–6, on the back of great players such as twins Kerrod and Kevin Walters, Steve Renouf, Glenn Lazarus, Chris Johns and their little captain 'Alfie' Langer.

The Broncos, however, are a privately-owned franchise and their owners came into conflict with Sydney-based League officials. Their dissatisfaction with the way the game was being run directly led to Brisbane's involvement in a rebel Super League in the mid-1990s.

Above: Paul Vautin.

State of Origin: 'Fatty's Heroes', 1995

State of Origin in the 1990s became an almighty contest that drew in huge amounts of fans and sponsorship money to the game. The Blues won six series that decade, with matches becoming known for the speed, hard hits and Queensland fightbacks. The League also tested Victoria's interest in the game with several matches drawing huge crowds to the MCG.

With Super League players banned from representative matches in 1995 and 1996, NSW looked to be the overwhelming favourites, but the plucky Maroons, under first-time coach Paul Vautin, won the 1995 series 3 games to nil! NSW bounced back to win in 1996, while 1997 saw a rebel interstate series conducted by Super League.

Below: Brisbane Broncos' 1993 premiership-winning team captained by Allan Langer (front row, centre).

1990s

The Canberra Raiders: 'The Green Machine' 1990–1994

The Canberra Raiders of the early 90s dominated their opponents. In the 1990s, the club missed the finals only once (in 1992) and played in three grand finals, winning two. Their dominance placed their teams alongside the great Easts, Manly, Parramatta and Canterbury teams of the modern era.

Coached by former Penrith mentor Tim Sheens, Canberra won their maiden premiership in 1989 and were too classy for the Panthers in the 1990 grand final. Captain Mal Meninga, Ricky Stuart, Laurie Daley, Steve Walters and Gary Belcher were at the peak of their Test careers, but injuries and salary cap breaching penalties saw them lose to a spirited Penrith team in the 1991 grand final, 19–12.

In 1994, Meninga's last season as a player, Canberra blitzed the competition and then belted the Bulldogs 36–12 in the grand final. This was the last time the Raiders won the competition.

MAL MENINGA: 'BIG MAL'

Mal Meninga had a stellar career which spanned three decades and saw him become the only player to be picked in four Kangaroo Tours (1982, 1986, 1990 and 1994). 'Big Mal' kicked 7 goals in the first State of Origin game played in 1980. The following year, the Queensland star turned down a big offer to play with the Roosters, opting to stay in Brisbane. In 1982, he earnt his first Test jumper, but dislocated his elbow on debut. At the end of the year he toured with the Kangaroos and cemented his place in the Test side.

Meninga joined the Raiders in 1986 and the following year they made the grand final for the first time, losing to Manly. During the 1990 season, he scored 38 points against Easts with 5 tries and 9 goals – the second highest individual points tally in a game. He captained the Raiders to premiership success in 1989–90 and 1994.

'Big Mal' became Australian Test captain in 1990, following the broken arm injury suffered by Wally Lewis. Meninga led the Kangaroos to England and France in 1990 and 1994, the only player to captain two tours, and retained the Ashes on both occasions.

Mal had a reasonable but short career as coach of Canberra before leading Queensland to its most dominant era in Interstate football (tens wins between 2006–16). He has since moved on to coaching the Kangaroos and led them to World Cup success in 2017.

The Last of the Kangaroo Tours, 1990 and 1994

After the dominance of the 1982 and 1986 Kangaroos, Australia's 1990 touring side was expected to continue the trend. They dominated in their tour games but were outclassed by Great Britain in the first Test, going down 19–12. Australia won the remaining two Tests in what was an extremely close and exciting series. Mal Meninga scored a great try off a Ricky Stuart run in the second Test to keep the series alive. Australia then blitzed France racking up some huge scores.

The 1994 Kangaroos were the last full genuine tour to date and again Australia were expected to go through the tour undefeated. Just as happened in the 1990 tour, however, Great Britain won the first Test in a boil over. It was the only game Australia lost on tour as they blitzed every opponent after that game, winning the Ashes series comfortably and then belting their French opponents by massive scores.

Australia proved unbeatable in the 1990s, winning the Ashes at home in 1992 and beating the Kiwis and Great Britain in Tri-Nation and Trans-Tasman competitions.

The Super League Split, 1997

Plans for a breakaway competition were first suggested in the late 1980s but it wasn't until a sponsorship argument between the Broncos and the Brisbane Rugby League saw the club relocate to the QEII Stadium (ANZ Stadium) and brought matters to a head. Broncos CEO John Ribot thought the ARL was not running the game properly and he found a willing backer in media mogul Rupert Murdoch, the owner of News Ltd.

In 1995, Super League made its move, signing clubs *en masse* and certain star players. Court action in 1996 put the rebels on hold but the following year, the game was split asunder. The Super League competition kicked off in 1997 with the addition of two new clubs, Adelaide and Hunter (Newcastle), alongside former ARL clubs Auckland, Brisbane, Cronulla, Canterbury, Canberra, Cowboys, Penrith and Perth.

Super League conducted a rebel competition, rival interstate series (also including New Zealand!) and internationals, and a farcical club challenge competition against the English Super League. Millions of dollars were wasted but by the time the two Leagues reunited in 1998, the ARL had lost control of the game.

Below: Ricky Stuart playing for Australia in 1990.

1990s

New ARL Clubs, 1995

Auckland (later NZ) Warriors
North Queensland Cowboys
South Queensland Crushers
Western Reds (later Perth Reds)

Super League Clubs, 1997

Adelaide Rams formed
Hunter Mariners formed

NRL Clubs, 1998

Melbourne Storm formed
Hunter Mariners (out)
Western Reds (out)
South Queensland (out)

NRL Coming and Goings, 1999

St George and Illawarra merged, playing as St George-Illawarra.
Adelaide Rams (out)
Gold Coast Chargers (out)
South Sydney was excluded from the NRL at the end of the 1999 season.

NRL Amalgamations for 2000

Western Suburbs and Balmain merged at the end of the 1999 season, playing as the Wests Tigers in 2000.
Manly and North Sydney merged at the end of the 1999 season, playing as the Northern Eagles in 2000.

Did You Know?

The Kangaroos that competed in the Centenary World Cup in 1995 represented the Australian Rugby League, which meant any players who had aligned with Super League were not selected. This decision saw a host of Test stars overlooked and a much younger and inexperienced side selected. Captained by Brad Fittler, Australia still won the World Cup final, 14–6.

Pay TV in the 1990s: 'The Media Wars'

Super League was the brainchild of billionaire Rupert Murdoch, who owns News Ltd, Foxtel, Fox News and 21st Century Fox. The plan essentially was to have Rugby League shown entirely on his subscription television network, Foxtel. The problem, however, was the Kerry Packer-owned Nine Network had the free-to-air TV rights to the game and refused to share them. Super League thus organised its own competition to have access to Rugby League games on their Pay TV network.

1997 ARL Premiership Table

Team	P	W	L	D	F	A	Pts
Manly	22	15	5	2	521	366	32
Newcastle	22	14	7	1	512	320	29
Parramatta	22	14	7	1	431	359	29
Norths	22	13	8	1	529	341	27
Sydney City	22	13	8	1	487	366	27
Illawarra	22	10	9	3	423	376	23
Gold Coast	22	10	11	1	438	466	21
Balmain	22	10	12	0	339	340	20
Wests	22	10	12	0	355	424	20
St George	22	9	12	1	331	392	19
Souths	22	4	17	1	323	630	9
South Qld	22	4	18	0	321	630	8

1997 Super League Premiership Table

Team	P	W	L	D	F	A	Pts
Brisbane	18	14	3	1	481	283	29
Cronulla	18	12	6	0	403	230	24
Canberra	18	11	7	0	436	337	22
Canterbury	18	10	8	0	453	447	20
Penrith	18	9	9	0	431	462	18
Hunter	18	7	11	0	350	363	14
Auckland	18	7	11	0	332	406	14
Perth	18	7	11	0	321	456	14
Adelaide	18	6	11	1	303	402	13
North Qld	18	5	11	2	328	452	12

Above: The respective League tables from the rival competitions in 1997 – 22 teams in all!

Above: The Newcastle Knights celebrate their win over Manly in the 1997 ARL grand final.

Two competitions; two grand finals, 1997

In the 1997 Super League grand final, Brisbane defeated Cronulla 26–8 at Brisbane's ANZ Stadium in front of a record Queensland crowd of 58,912. The match was played at night (and it rained) but it did nothing but reinforce the belief that Super League had been set up to favour the Broncos.

In Sydney, the Paul Harragon-led Newcastle Knights reached their first grand final but had to face a mighty Manly side, who were defending premiers. Manly lead 16–8 at halftime and, with six minutes remaining, were still up 16–10 but a great try by Robbie O'Davis, converted by Andrew Johns, levelled the scores. Right on fulltime, Johns made a break down the sideline and put his winger Darren Albert over for the winning try, 22–16, delivering Newcastle their first ever title.

1990s

The NRL Premiership trophy.

The Birth of the NRL, 1998

After the messy 1997 season where both the ARL and Super League conducted rival competitions, both factions realised that working together would be beneficial to all Rugby League fans. In December of that year, the two Leagues made peace and set about unifying the competition.

The biggest problem was the large number of clubs. Super League had 10 teams while the ARL had 12. Starting with 20 teams in 1998, they agreed to cut clubs and force amalgamations over the next three seasons, working towards a competition of 14 teams for the 2000 season.

This battle was ugly and ran for several years, but it also provided great innovation into how the game was broadcast. Super League's video referee system was retained, with games televised on Channel 9 and Foxtel, while the newly formed National Rugby League (NRL) featured administrators from both competitions to run the game.

BRAD FITTLER: 'BOY TO MAN'

Brad Fittler was a star from his very first season in the game. The big-stepping centre made his debut for Penrith in 1989, aged 18, and appeared in both of the club's finals appearances. In 1990, he was selected for NSW, making him the youngest Origin player at the time, and also played in his first grand final. At the end of the season, he became the youngest Australian representative when selected for the Kangaroos.

In 1991, Fittler earnt his first Test jumper and then won a premiership with Penrith, going on to achieve the unbelievable career feat of playing in State of Origin, Tests, a World Cup Final (1992) and a grand final win before turning 21 years old. He was a prime target for Super League when Penrith sided with the rival competition, but the ARL made him Test captain and Fittler led Australia to Trans-Tasman and World Cup success in 1995.

Fittler chose to leave the Panthers and sided with the ARL-aligned Roosters in 1996. His arrival coincided with Easts most successful period since the Jack Gibson era in the 1970s. He captained the Roosters to the premiership in 2002 before retiring in 2004. He briefly coached the Roosters from 2007–09 before taking on media duties and being named NSW coach in 2018.

The 1999 Grand Final: Melbourne v St George Illawarra

The 1999 grand final between the Melbourne Storm and St George Illawarra was historic for many reasons. The first time two sides met in the decider having never even played in a grand final before, the match also drew a world record Rugby League crowd with 107,999 people filling the newly built Sydney Olympic Stadium.

The match also ended amid great controversy when Storm winger Craig Smith was tackled high by Jamie Ainscough while fielding a kick in the St George Illawarra in-goal area in the dying stages of the game. The Dragons led 18–14 at the time, having led 14–0 nil at one stage of the match, but the Storm were awarded a penalty try after Smith was knocked senseless by Ainscough while trying to ground the ball for the try.

Being a penalty try, the Storm converted the try from in front of the posts and won the match 20–18. Storm captain Glenn Lazarus became the first to win premierships with three clubs (also Canberra, 1989–90 and Brisbane, 1992–93).

Above: Melbourne Storm captain Glenn Lazarus.
Left: Nathan Blacklock scoots away for a try.
Below: Storm players at the end of the 1999 grand final.

2000s

The Premiers

2000 Grand Final
Brisbane 14 • Sydney Roosters 6

2001 Grand Final
Newcastle 30 • Parramatta 24

2002 Grand Final
Sydney Roosters 30 • NZ Warriors 8

2003 Grand Final
Penrith 18 • Sydney Roosters 6

2004 Grand Final
Bulldogs 16 • Sydney Roosters 13

2005 Grand Final
Wests Tigers 30 • Cowboys 16

2006 Grand Final
Brisbane 15 • Melbourne 8

2007 Grand Final
Melbourne 34 • Manly 8*

2008 Grand Final
Manly 40 • Melbourne 0

2009 Grand Final
Melbourne 23 • Parramatta 16*

* Melbourne Storm were stripped of these premierships due to salary cap breaches

Team Changes
Gold Coast Titans entered in 2007.

Did You Know?

Melbourne were the second team to win a premiership while over the salary cap. The first was Canberra in 1990, who were also the first team to breach the salary cap, but unlike Melbourne Canberra were not stripped of their title.

Panthers Pounce Again, 2003

In 2001, Penrith finished with the wooden spoon, which resulted in coach and club legend Royce Simmons being replaced by John Lang. Lang spent 2002 rebuilding the club and brought in Joe Galuvao, Martin Lang, Luke Priddis, Paul Whatuira, Ben Ross, Scott Sattler and Preston Campbell, while future Test stars Joel Clinton, Trent Waterhouse, Luke Lewis and Luke Rooney also made their debuts.

A confident, attacking powerhouse led by Test halfback Craig Gower and featuring prolific point-scorer Ryan Girdler finished top of the 2003 NRL table. Penrith defeated the more fancied Roosters, 18–6, in the grand final in a match featuring Scott Sattler's famous sideline tackle to turn the tide of the match.

Roosters Crow, 2000–2004

In 1995, Eastern Suburbs changed their name to Sydney City Roosters, which coincided with a dramatic improvement in their performances. In 1996 they secured Brad Fittler, who led the club to the finals in every season from 1996 to 2004. The club also made four grand finals in five years, winning only one.

In 2000, the Roosters reached their first grand final since 1980, but lost to the Broncos, 14–6. In 2002, Ricky Stuart was in charge of the club when they won their 12th premiership by defeating the Warriors 30–8. Although the Roosters made the next two grand finals, they lost to Penrith in 2003 and the Bulldogs in 2004, which was also Fittler's farewell to the game.

Above: Penrith's Scott Sattler's try-saving tackle of Todd Byrne in the 2003 grand final.

Wests Tigers, 2005: 'The Marshall Factor'

Future Kiwi Test captain Benji Marshall was still in high school in 2003 when he made his NRL debut for the Wests Tigers. In that game, he showed his footwork and acceleration, amazing everyone with his running and passing game. In 2004, he suffered the first of several shoulder injuries, but in 2005 his great form helped carry the club into their maiden finals campaign, where they beat the Cowboys in the grand final.

Wests Tigers had been major underperformers in the early 2000s before luring premiership-winning coach Tim Sheens to the club. With Marshall and former Broncos halfback Scott Prince leading the way, Wests Tigers beat the Cowboys 30–16 in a grand final that featured a stunning flick pass from Marshall to winger Pat Richards that led to one of the game's most exciting tries.

Left: Benji Marshall playing for the Wests Tigers in the 2005 grand final.

2000s

South Sydney: 'The Fightback, 2000–2002'

October 15, 1999 was a sad day for Rugby League when the NRL's rationalisation plans saw foundation club South Sydney being informed that they would not be included in the 2000 competition after failing to satisfy criteria to determine a club's financial stability and success.

Although the 1990s were the most disappointing in the Rabbitohs' long and proud history, club boss George Piggins refused to let the club fold or be merged. When the NRL axed the club, he fought valiantly through the courts to have Souths reinstated.

On July 6, 2001, the High Court ruled that Souths had been illegally excluded by the NRL. The NRL opted not to contest the decision and agreed to return Souths to the competition in 2002. Their first game back was in the pre-season Charity Shield match against St George Illawarra, which resulted in a 20–all draw. Hard days lay ahead when they lost their opening NRL match to arch foes the Sydney Roosters, but 35,316 fans turned out to support the club. Souths were back!

ANDREW JOHNS: 'THE GREATEST EVER'?

Andrew Johns combined the vision of Duncan Thompson and Peter Sterling, the passing game of Keith Holman, the running and stepping game of Allan Langer and the kicking game of Ricky Stuart. A match-winner with the boot, he may have lacked the pace of traditional darting halfbacks but he could hit the defensive line hard and could tackle with the intensity of a forward.

Johns made his debut with the Knights in 1993 and scored a club record 23 points in his first full match (a record he would later better). His breakout season was in 1995, helping Newcastle to reach the finals and earning selection for NSW Country, New South Wales and Australia. At the end of the year, he starred in Australia's World Cup win, but often had to play hooker in rep teams in ensuing years because of the number of good halfbacks in the game.

Johns set up the match winning try right on fulltime to deliver the Knights their first ever premiership in 1997 (brother Matty Johns was also in that team). Four years later, he was the architect of Newcastle's upset win over Parramatta in the 2001 grand final.

'Joey' Johns could do it all – he won the Dally M medal in 1998, 1999 and 2002, and was a two-time Golden Boot award winner (1999 and 2001). In 2006, he broke the record for most career points and retired in 2007 as arguably the greatest player the game has ever seen. His selection in Australia's 'Team of the Century' at halfback in 2008 added weight to that view.

The Internationals, 2000s

In an effort to promote the international game after the Super League split, international Rugby League promoted Tri-Nation, Four Nation and World Cup competitions in the late 1990s and early 2000s.

Led by Brad Fittler, Australia dominated the 2000 World Cup and won the last two Ashes series ever played, in 2001 and 2003 (led by Darren Lockyer). The Kangaroos also won the 2004 and 2006 Tri Nation competitions; however, they lost the 2005 Tri Nations final to New Zealand.

The Kangaroos were again thwarted by New Zealand in the 2008 World Cup final and lost their World Number 1 ranking to the Kiwis. Australia closed out the decade by winning the first ever Four-Nations tournament in 2009, defeating New Zealand, England and France.

Below: Australia wins the 2000 World Cup.

Above: Andrew Johns playing for Australia, 2001.

2000s

Australia in the World Cup

2000 in Great Britain and France

Round 1 – won 22–2 v England
Round 2 – won 66–8 v Fiji
Round 3 – won 110–4 v Russia
Quarter Final – won 66–10 v Samoa
Semi Final – won 46–22 v Wales
Final – won 40–12 v New Zealand

2008 in Australia

Round 1 – won 30–6 v NZ
Round 2 – won 52–4 v England
Round 3 – won 46–6 v Papua New Guinea
Semi Final – won 52–0 v Fiji
Final – lost 34–20 v New Zealand

Other Internationals

2004 Tri-Nations Final

won v Great Britain, 44–4

2005 Tri-Nations Final

lost v New Zealand, 24–0

2006 Tri-Nations Final

won v New Zealand, 16–12*

* golden point extra time

2009 Four Nations Final

won v Great Britain, 46–16

Did You Know?

Australia were hot favourites in the 2008 World Cup – a competition to highlight the 100th anniversary of Rugby League in this country – and were undefeated in the preliminary rounds. In the 'upset of the century', however, the Ricky Stuart-coached Kangaroos lost the final to New Zealand, 34–20. It was the Kiwis' first ever World Cup Final victory.

Maroons Begin their Dominance, 2006

When Andrew Johns came back from injury to inspire NSW to an unlikely win in the 2005 State of Origin series, many were signalling the death of interstate football. The public had lost interest, the media said. The concept was dead.

Queensland responded as only the Maroons can, and reeled off series wins in the next eight years – 2006 to 2013. Coached by Mal Meninga and led by Darren Lockyer in the early years of this run, the Maroons greatly benefited from Melbourne's 'Fab Four' and an emerging North Queensland champion named Johnathan Thurston – and an undeniable will to win.

The Melbourne Storm: 'A Decade of Success'

The Melbourne Storm were formed by the NRL in 1998, made up largely by players from the disbanded Hunter, Adelaide and Western Reds clubs. Wearing the colours of purple, gold and royal blue, the Storm made the finals in their debut season and won their first premiership the following year.

After poor seasons in 2001–02, the Storm signed coach, Craig Bellamy, and uncovered some young talent from Queensland. Hooker Cameron Smith (who started his career as a halfback in 2002) was joined by Billy Slater (2003), Cooper Cronk (2004) and Greg Inglis (2005) to form the club's 'Fab Four'.

Melbourne reached the 2006 grand final but were 15–8 losers to Brisbane. The Storm then dominated 2007, belting Manly 34–8 in the grand final. They lost the 2008 decider by a record 40–0 margin against Manly – largely because of the suspension of Storm captain Cameron Smith for a dangerous tackle – but bounced back in the 2009 decider to defeat underdogs the Eels.

Manly v Melbourne: 'The Rivalry'

One of the most passionate and fiercely fought rivalries in modern times has been between Manly and Melbourne. Both teams became the benchmark for NRL success between 2007 and 2011, with each winning two premierships.

Manly made their return to the NRL in 2002 after three seasons as part of the failed Northern Eagles joint venture with rivals North Sydney. Under the coaching of former clubman Des Hasler, the Sea Eagles returned to finals football in 2005 and 2006, before becoming the only side capable of competing with the Storm. Manly were thumped by Melbourne in the 2007 grand final, but hit back with a 40–0 hiding of the Storm to claim the title in 2008. Their rivalry would continue into the new decade, with Manly winning the premiership in 2011 and Melbourne in 2012.

Above: Glenn Stewart charges through the Melbourne defence in the 2007 grand final.

Left: Queensland's Gorden Tallis takes on the NSW defence in the early 2000s.

2000s

The Centenary of Australian Rugby League, 2008

In 2008, the NRL celebrated the 100th anniversary of Rugby League in Australia. In February, a list of the 100 greatest players from the game's first century were named by a large panel of former players, coaches, administrators, journalists, commentators and historians. On April 17, the panel then selected the Team of the Century.

The team was: **Clive Churchill, Ken Irvine, Mal Meninga, Reg Gasnier, Brian Bevan, Wally Lewis, Andrew Johns, John Raper, Ron Coote, Norm Provan, Duncan Hall, Noel Kelly, Arthur Beetson.** Interchange: **Graeme Langlands, Bob Fulton, Dally Messenger, Frank Burge.** Coach: **Jack Gibson.**

Winger Brian Bevan was selected in the greatest ever Australian team despite playing most of his career in England!

DARREN LOCKYER: 'LOCKY'

Darren Lockyer's ability to change his game and still remain one of the best players in the world is a testament to just how great a player he was. Aged 18, he made his debut for the Broncos in 1995 as a five-eighth but, by 1997, he moved to fullback and became an instant star. He made his debut for the Queensland and Australian Super League teams that year while also playing in Brisbane's grand final win over Cronulla.

Lockyer's rapid improvement as a player and quiet leadership style saw him retain his place at State and Test level when the competitions reunited in 1998, and he became Test captain in 2003 following the retirement of Brad Fittler. He was awarded the Golden Boot as the best player in the world that year while playing as a fullback.

'Locky' moved back to five-eighth in 2004 and led the Broncos to grand final success in 2006. Australia's international success saw him secure his second Golden Boot award, making him the first player to do so from two different positions. He retired in 2011 after playing more club games than any other player (355), scoring most points for the Broncos (1195pts), as well as becoming the most capped Test player (55 Tests), most capped Test captain (38 Tests) and also top try-scorer in Tests (35 tries).

'Salary Cap' Breaches in the Modern Game

The enforcement of a 'salary cap' by the NRL – a cap on the amount of money each club can spend each year - has resulted in a tremendous 'evening' of the competition. But with rapidly inflated player salaries, however, some clubs felt pressured to retain their star players and chose to cheat the cap in an attempt to be successful.

The first of the big breaches came in 2002 by the Bulldogs, which resulted in the club losing all of the 37 competition points they had accumulated and saw them drop from first to last on the competition ladder. In 2005, the Warriors were caught breaching the cap and had to start the 2006 season on minus 4 competition points, which was enough to deny them a place in the finals.

2010 saw the biggest breach of all. The Melbourne Storm were found to have cheated the cap every year from 2006–2010. This resulted in the harshest penalties of all, with the 2007 and 2009 premierships, the 2006–2008 minor premierships and the 2010 World Club Challenge title stripped from the record books. It was a harsh blow to the integrity of the game.

It appears some clubs have been slow to learn from these breaches. In 2016, Parramatta were stripped of their Auckland Nines title and lost 12 competition points for breaching the salary cap, which also denied them a place in the finals that year.

Below: Captain Cameron Smith and coach Craig Bellamy (centre) lead the Melbourne Storm players out to face the media in 2010 after learning they had been stripped of their premiership wins in 2007 and 2009 because of salary cap breaches. Coach and players denied they had any direct knowledge of the club's salary cap rorting.

2010s

The Premiers

2010 Grand Final
St George Illawarra 32 • Sydney Roosters 8

2011 Grand Final
Manly 24 • NZ Warriors 10

2012 Grand Final
Melbourne 14 • Bulldogs 4

2013 Grand Final
Sydney Roosters 26 • Manly 18

2014 Grand Final
South Sydney 30 • Bulldogs 6

2015 Grand Final
Cowboys 17 • Brisbane 16*
* in golden point extra time

2016 Grand Final
Cronulla 14 • Melbourne 12

2017 Grand Final
Melbourne 34 • Cowboys 6

2018 Grand Final
Sydney Roosters 21 • Melbourne 6

2019 Grand Final
Sydney Roosters 14 • Canberra 8

Did You Know?

In late 2017, the Cronulla Sharks became the first team to have three players in their team who had each played at least 300 club games. They were Luke Lewis, Chris Heighington and Paul Gallen.

That year, there were six players in the NRL with at least 300 games experience. The others were Cameron Smith, Cooper Cronk and Ryan Hoffman, while Johnathan Thurston and Billy Slater finished the year on 299 games each.

Above: Father and son Dean Young (2010) and Craig Young (1977, 1979) both won premierships with the Dragons during their respective careers.

St George Illawarra, 2010: 'Success at Last!'

In the decade after 1999, merged club St George Illawarra had been relatively successful without making the grand final. In 2009 they signed successful Broncos coach Wayne Bennett and the club achieved almost immediate success.

Bennett took the Dragons to their first ever minor premiership in 2009, a feat repeated in 2010. Unlike 2009, however, where the Dragons lost both finals matches, 2010 saw the club go all the way to the grand final where they decimated the Roosters, 32–8, to claim their first title.

St George fans had waited 31 years for grand final success, but Bennett left the club at the end of the next year for Newcastle. St George Illawarra reached the finals just once in the next six seasons.

Souths, 2014: 'The Rabbitohs break through'

South Sydney struggled in their first five years after being readmitted to the NRL in 2002, but the club was revitalised when actor Russell Crowe and businessman Peter Holmes à Court took over the running of the club and started to attract key players such as Greg Inglis and the Burgess brothers.

The appointment of coach Michael Maguire turned the Rabbitohs into a top NRL team in 2012. After making the preliminary final in three consecutive years, Souths qualified for their first grand final in 43 years and took on the Bulldogs.

After a tense battle, Souths won 30–6 to claim their first title since 1971. Forward Sam Burgess played most of the match with a fractured cheekbone and won the Clive Churchill Medal for his efforts. Souths had come a long way in just over a decade back in the NRL.

Cowboys v Brisbane, 2015: 'Thurston's Golden Point'

In 2015, the Cowboys reached their second grand final and met local rivals Brisbane in a game that has since been regarded as the greatest finish to a grand final ever – even better than the 1989 grand final between Balmain and Canberra, perhaps.

Brisbane led 14–12 at the break but, after adding a goal, they tried to 'close out' the game in the second half. A last minute try to Cowboys winger Kyle Feldt, off a desperate Michael Morgan pass, tied the scores at 16–all as fulltime sounded.

Johnathan Thurston's sideline conversion then hit the upright, forcing the game into extra time. After the first scrum, Thurston kicked a field goal to give the Cowboys their first ever premiership. It was a breathtaking finish to one of the best grand finals ever.

Below: The North Queensland Cowboys celebrate their golden point extra-time win over arch-rivals Brisbane in the 2015 grand final. Johnathan Thurston kicked a field goal to clinch the Cowboys' first title, 17–16.

2010s

State of Origin, 2010s: 'Queensland's dominance continues'

In 2010, Queensland made a clean sweep of the Origin series with possibly the greatest State side assembled – Darius Boyd, Petero Civoniceva, Cooper Cronk, Israel Folau, Ben Hannant, Greg Inglis, Darren Lockyer, Nate Myles, Matt Scott, David Shillington, Billy Slater, Cameron Smith, Sam Thaiday, Johnathan Thurston and Willie Tonga – all of them Test stars.

Under Mal Meninga's coaching, Queensland won the next three series as well, making it eight straight before a gallant Blues outfit, led by Paul Gallen and coached by Laurie Daley, ended the run in 2014. The Maroons bounced back to win in 2015 and didn't miss a beat under new coach Kevin Walters, winning both the 2016 and 2017 series against the more-fancied NSW team.

JOHNATHAN THURSTON: 'JT'

The greatest current day halfback is unquestionably Johnathan Thurston. 'JT' has won almost every award on offer, as well as captained the Cowboys to a premiership (2015), inspired Queensland to a record number of Origin wins (2006–2017) and captured three Golden Boot awards (2011, 2013 and 2015) as the best player in the world.

Thurston made his first-grade debut with the Bulldogs in 2002, where he won a premiership with the club in 2004 before being lured to the Cowboys. His first full season as the chief playmaker propelled the Cowboys to their first ever grand final appearance in 2005, but they were no match for the Wests Tigers. Thurston earnt himself a place in the Maroons Origin squad that year and was named the Dally M player of the year for the first of a record four times.

'JT' made his Test debut in 2006 and appeared in a record 37 consecutive State of Origin matches before injury ended his 'rep' career in 2017. In this time, Queensland were beaten only once in an Origin series (2014).

In 2015, he led the Cowboys to their first ever Premiership, kicking the match winning field goal in extra time against the Broncos and winning the Clive Churchill Medal as man of the match. 'JT' retired at the end of the 2018 season after playing over 300 games with 2222 points to his credit at club level.

The Pacific Explosion!

Ever since the game's birth, there have been players from other countries lining up to play for Rugby League clubs. At times, bans were put in place in Australia and England to restrict players from either country from going overseas, so as to ensure their local competitions remained strong. In Australia, this saw clubs look elsewhere for talent, with Pacific Island nations the most heavily targeted. In the late 1960s, Apisai Toga was one of the first players from the region to become a regular first grade player, spending five years at the Dragons before his tragic death cut his career short in 1973.

The introduction of the Auckland Warriors in 1995 opened the floodgates to the Pacific region, with players from New Zealand, Samoa, Tonga, Fiji, Cook Islands, Vanuatu and Solomon Islands finding their way into the elite competition. Today, the game has players from the most diverse range of nationalities taking place in the NRL, which has seen a dramatic improvement in the quality of International football in the Southern Hemisphere, as evidenced by the success of Tonga, Fiji and Samoa in the 2017 World Cup. The following year Australia played their first ever Test against Tonga, winning 34-16.

The Cronulla Sharks, 2016: 'Success, 50 seasons in the making'

The Cronulla Sharks held the most unwanted record in the game's history having never won a title since coming into the League in 1967. They had made just three grand finals, losing twice to Manly, in 1973 and 1978, and then falling to the Broncos in the 1997 Super League competition.

The Sharks were often besieged with off-field controversies and financial drama, most notably the investigation into performance enhancing substance use in 2013–14. The Sharks cleaned out their administration, secured their financial future and built a highly professional team. In 2016 they set a club record 15 straight wins to reach the grand final.

Led by NSW captain Paul Gallen, Cronulla were too fast and determined for the Melbourne Storm, winning a nail-biter, 14–12, to end their premiership drought.

Right: Cronulla Sharks players celebrate the club's inaugural grand final win in 2016.

2010s

Australia in the World Cup

2013 in Great Britain and France

Round 1 – won 28–20 v England
Round 2 – won 34–2 v Fiji
Round 3 – won 50–0 v Ireland
Quarter Final – won 62–0 v USA
Semi Final – won 64–0 v Fiji
Final – won 34–2 v New Zealand

2017 in Australia, New Zealand and Papua New Guinea

Round 1 – won 18–4 v England
Round 2 – won 52–6 v France
Round 3 – won 34–0 v Lebanon
Quarter Final – won 46–0 v Samoa
Semi Final – won 54–6 v Fiji
Final – won 6–0 v England

Other Internationals

2010 Four Nations Final
lost v New Zealand, 16–12

2011 Four Nations Final
won v Great Britain, 30–8

2014 Four Nations Final
lost v New Zealand, 22–18

2016 Four Nations Final
won v New Zealand, 34–8

Did You Know?

New Zealand defeated Australia in three successive Tests in 2014–15. The Kiwis, inspired by halfback Shaun Johnson, defeated the Kangaroos in the opening match of the 2014 Four Nations competition in Brisbane, 30–12, and then backed up to win the final in Wellington (NZ). The following year, they won the early season Test in Brisbane, 26–12.

Above: Storm captain Cameron Smith after the 2017 grand final.

The Storm, 2017 'Back on Top!'

The 2017 grand final saw the all-conquering Melbourne Storm take on eighth-placed North Queensland in a real 'David and Goliath' match. The Storm bounced back from the narrow loss to Cronulla in the 2016 decider to win the minor premiership the following year.

The club also welcomed back champion fullback Billy Slater after missing most of the previous two years with serious injuries. Led by Cameron Smith, and riding on the emotion of Cooper Cronk's final game for the club, the Storm flogged the Cowboys 34–6 to be hailed the best team of the modern era.

The 'Immortals'

In 1981, *Rugby League Week* chose the four greatest post-World War II players as part of a promotion. The four 'Immortals' were selected by noted commentator Frank Hyde, successful coach Harry Bath and long-time journalist Tom Goodman. The selectors could only choose players they had seen and this is why pre-war pioneers were not considered.

The original four players selected were Clive Churchill, Reg Gasnier, John Raper and Bob Fulton. Graeme Langlands and Wally Lewis were added in 1999, and the selection of Arthur Beetson (2003) and Andrew Johns (2012) brought the number of Immortals to eight. In 2018, the NRL honoured pre-War stars 'Dally' Messenger, Frank Burge and Dave Brown, along with Norm Provan and Mal Meninga. In 2024 Ron Coote was named the 14th 'Immortal'.

Below: Andrew Johns.

WAYNE BENNETT: 'MODERN DAY SUPERCOACH'

Queenslander Wayne Bennett has coached more 1st grade games than any other coach in the code's history. A talented winger who represented Queensland and Australia (1971), Bennett first captain-coached Ipswich in 1976 and was still going strong 40 years later. He coached Canberra to the 1987 grand final (with Don Furner) before returning to Brisbane to coach the Broncos for a record 21 consecutive years (1988–2008). He moved to St George Illawarra in 2009 and won a premiership there (2010) before three moderately successful years at Newcastle (2012–14). In 2015, he returned to the Broncos where he later passed the 800 game mark before being named Souths coach for 2019.

Bennett first coached Queensland in 1986, but had greater success in the late 1990s and early 2000s as coach of Brisbane, Queensland and Australia. In 2008, he was coaching advisor to the Kiwis in their shock World Cup win over Australia and, in 2017, coached England to the World Cup final.

A man of few words but a dry wit, Bennett loves the game. Perhaps his greatest ability is not only reinventing Rugby League teams, but getting the best out of the players at his disposal.

2010s

The 2017 World Cup: 'Australia World Champions'

In 2017, the World Cup was held in Australia and saw games also played in Papua New Guinea for the first time, as well as New Zealand. The Cup was dominated by teams from the Southern Hemisphere, with Papua New Guinea, Tonga, Fiji and Australia winning all three of their pool games, while New Zealand won twice.

Lebanon appeared in their first World Cup and were surprisingly good, making their way to quarter finals and very nearly beating heavyweight side Tonga.

Cronulla and Australian winger/fullback

Above: Australian captain Cameron Smith, 2017.

Valentine Holmes was the star of the finals when he scored five tries against Samoa and then crossed for six tries against Fiji the following week. Australia beat England in a hard-fought final, 6–0, to claim their 11th World Cup success and their first success on home soil since 1977.

CAMERON SMITH: 'CAPTAIN COURAGEOUS'

Cameron Smith will undoubtedly be regarded as the greatest hooker in the game's history. His ability to control the ruck from dummy half, his unbelievable endurance and durability, play making skills, vision and utter professionalism sees him as the most elite player in a long time.

Smith debuted with the Storm in 2002 after coming from Norths Brisbane. He played two games at halfback before transitioning into the hooker role the following year, where he blossomed so quickly that he was called into the Queensland team for Game 3 of the 2003 series. He has been a regular 'rep' player ever since.

2006 saw his career go to another level, making his Test debut, playing in the Storm's losing grand final team and being named the Dally M player of the year. In 2007 he was awarded the Golden Boot award as best international player. He made his Test debut as captain against New Zealand in 2007.

After the devastating decision by the NRL to strip the Storm of its 2007 and 2009 titles, Smith was integral in holding the club together and seeing them through the drama. He then led Melbourne back to premiership success in 2012, and again in 2017.

By the end of the 2017 season, Cameron Smith had broken many records – notably, most 1st grade games, most career goals at club level and most Origin appearances. He retired from representative football in 2018 to focus purely on club games. He led the Storm to Grand Final appearances in 2018 and 2020, and despite failing to win in 2018, he was able to bow out of the game with another Premiership ring in his last match, when Melbourne beat Penrith 26-20 in the 2020 Grand Final.

Women in League: Jillaroos and the NRLW

Women and young girls have always been among Rugby League's most devoted fans. Although females have long been involved in touch football, OZtag and junior League competitions around the country, and many have opted to be part of the administration of the game, there were few opportunities for women to play League at an elite level.

The Australian Jillaroos first competed in a Test match against New Zealand in 1995. By 2013, they were crowned World Cup champions, and also competed in State of Origin, All Stars and Auckland Nines competition.

In 2017, the Jillaroos defeated the Kiwi Ferns in the Women's Rugby League World Cup, 23–16, after being given double-header billing with the Australia-England RLWC decider at Suncorp Stadium. Australia now boasts World Championships in both men's and women's Rugby League.

2018 saw the debut of the NRL Women's competition. It comprised of four teams; Brisbane Broncos, St George-Illawarra Dragons, Sydney Roosters and the Warriors. The Broncos won the first Women's RL Grand Final, 34-12, over the Roosters.

Right: Sam Bremner.

Fittler's Blues, 2018

After years of Queensland dominance at interstate level, coach Brad Fittler led NSW to its first State of Origin series win 2014 and just their second series win since 2006! This was Queensland's most dominant era in interstate football since 1908. The Blues' success may have coincided with the 'rep' retirement of star Maroons players Cameron Smith, Johnathan Thurston and Cooper Cronk, but there was no denying the enthusiasm of the fresh-faced NSW team in 2018.

NSW won the series in the opening two matches – 22-12 in Melbourne and 18-14 in Sydney – before losing the 'dead rubber' in Brisbane, 18-12. Nevertheless, Fittler's fresh approach brought immediate results and hopefully heralded a new era of success for the Blues.

Cooper Cronk Inspires Roosters, 2018

At the beginning of the 2018 season, long-time Melbourne Storm halfback Cooper Cronk surprised everyone by signing a two-year contract with the Sydney Roosters. The Roosters slowly built momentum during the season, learning to play a new style under the guidance of the veteran Cronk, but by the end of the year they finished top of the League table with a better 'for and against' record. Facing his old club in the grand final, Cronk took a shoulder injury into the game and guided the Roosters to a comfortable 21-6 win over the Storm.

It was a courageous display from the little halfback, proving once again the old adage that League is a game where the little men can shine!

2020s

The Premiers

2020 Grand Final
Melbourne 26 • Penrith 20

2021 Grand Final
Penrith 14 • Souths 12

2022 Grand Final
Penrith 28 • Parramatta 12

2023 Grand Final
Penrith 26 • Brisbane 24

2024 Grand Final
Penrith 14 • Melbourne 6

Team Changes
Dolphins entered in 2023

Did You Know?

21 of the 26 Grand Finals played since 1998 have contained either the Melbourne Storm, Sydney Roosters or Penrith Panthers, yet despite this there have been 12 different clubs that have won a premiership in that time.

Covid shuts down Rugby League

In 2020, the Coronavirus pandemic finally reached Australia, however after the first round had been completed, the virus had spread around the country, forcing the Government to close all borders. The NRL played all of Round 2 in empty stadiums. The game then shut down all competition for 2 months.

When the competition resumed the NRL had decided to reduce the season length from 25 Rounds to 20, while State of Origin was moved to the end of the year, after the Grand Final. Rounds 3 and 4 were played in front of empty stadiums. Teams were placed in 'bubbles' where they were allowed severely restricted contact with other people. Teams shared venues to reduce travel and exposure to the virus. The New Zealand based Warriors side made the difficult decision to stay in Australia for the rest of the season, away from their loved ones.

Rounds 5 to 7 were almost entirely played in front of crowds of less than a thousand people. From Round 8 til Round 20 the crowd sizes were increased, but still at a significantly reduced capacity, with most games attended by less than 10,000 people. Week 3 of the finals saw crowds of over 30,000 for the first time all year, while the Grand Final was played in front of 37,303. State Of Origin was played over 3 consecutive weeks in November.

The 2021 season kicked off cautiously in March, with lockdowns of varying severity in place in all states at various times of the year. Crowds were still capped and players were still in their 'bubbles'. The Melbourne Storm based themselves on the Sunshine Coast for the entire season due to the severity of covid outbreaks in Victoria, which had put the state in the longest lockdowns in all of Australia, while the Warriors again spent the whole season in Australia. When Sydney got locked down in July, the NRL games played across the city were played in empty stadiums again. The NRL then hastily relocated to Queensland and just as they did so, that state went into lockdown and another near 2 rounds were played in empty stadiums.

The game remained in Queensland for the remainder of the year, with finals games in Week 1 played in Rockhampton, Townsville and the Sunshine Coast, Week 2 in Mackay and the remaining games, including the Grand Final, were all played at Suncorp Stadium in Brisbane.

The aftermath saw some changes to the game to try and cut down on costs. The two on-field referees reverted back to just one and players agreed to a 20% pay cut for the 2020 season.

Photo: Wikicommons / RegionalQueenslander

The Dolphins, preparing to play a QRL side in 2023.

Birth of the Dolphins

In September 2020, Queensland Cup club Redcliffe Dolphins, put in a bid to enter a separate side into the NRL and just over a year later, the NRL granted the Dolphins a licence to compete in the NRL starting in 2023. The club fought off bids from Perth and two others from Brisbane. They landed the key signing of Wayne Bennett as head coach who then built his roster for their debut season, landing key players Felise Kaufusi, Jesse and Kenny Bromwich, Tom Gilbert, Hamiso Tabuai-Fidow, Jamayne Isaako, Isaiya Katoa, Jeremy Marshall-King, Kodi Nikorima and Jarrod Wallace. Their debut season got off to a good start and they were inside the top 8 at the halfway point of the season, but their lack of depth saw them struggle in the second half of the year as they dropped down to 13th.

2024 was a much better season, but it was the second half of the year that hurt them again. At the end of the penultimate round of the year, they were in 8th place, but a last round loss to the Knights saw the Newcastle side jump into the top 8 while the Dolphins finished the year in 10th.

Panthers 4-Peat!

It had long been said how hard it was for any team to win back-to-back Premierships during the salary cap era, which began in 1990. Only the Brisbane Broncos of 1992–93 and the Sydney Roosters of 2018–19 managed to achieve the feat.

But then along came the Penrith Panthers. After making the finals in 2016, 2017 and 2018, In 2019 they fell just one win short of the top 8. In 2020, Penrith lost just one game all year to advance to the Grand Final, which they lost narrowly to Melbourne.

The Panthers again dominated in 2021, but suffered a surprise loss to Souths in the first week of the finals. Penrith bounced back to beat Parramatta and Melbourne in low scoring battles before returning the favour to Souths in the Grand Final, winning 14–12.

Penrith comfortably claimed the Minor Premiership in 2022, then beat Parramatta and Souths to advance to their third straight Grand Final, where they beat Parramatta 28–12.

Penrith were again Minor Premiers in 2023 and again strolled into the Grand Final on the back of convincing victories over the Warriors and Melbourne. The Broncos held a 4-point lead with just four minutes remaining in the match when Panthers halfback Nathan Cleary scored a try, which he converted to give the Panthers a last gasp 2-point victory and their third straight Premiership – the first time such a feat had happened since the brilliant Parramatta side of 1981–83.

In 2024 it was a resurgent Melbourne Storm who were Minor Premiers, with the Panthers in second place. Both teams had comfortably victories in their finals games to meet again in the Grand Final. Penrith were in their 5th straight Grand Final, the first side to do so since the Souths team of 1967–71. Penrith won a brilliant contest 14–6 to claim their 4th straight title, a feat last achieved by the Mighty Dragons side of 1956–66 who won 11 straight, while the champion South Sydney team from 1925–29 the only other side to win at least four straight titles.

2020s

Australia in the World Cup

2021 in England (played in 2022)
Round 1 – won 42–8 v Fiji
Round 2 – won 84–0 v Scotland
Round 3 – won 66–6 v Italy
Quarter Final – won 48–4 v Lebanon
Semi Final – won 16–14 v New Zealand
Final – won 30–10 v Samoa
Other Internationals
2023 Pacific Cup Final
lost v New Zealand, 0–30
2024 Pacific Cup Final
won v Tonga, 20–14

Rugby League goes to Las Vegas!

The 2024 season opened with a double-header played at the Allegiant Stadium in Las Vegas. Manly defeated Souths 36–24 in the first Premiership game ever played in America, before the Sydney Roosters beat the Brisbane Broncos 20–10 in the second match. A crowd of 40,746 people were in attendance for the event.

In 2025 the Raiders and Warriors will open the season at the same venue, before the Panthers and Sharks square off in the second match.

Australian Rugby League has flirted with spreading the sport to the United States as early as 1910. America has dabbled with the code sporadically over the years, but this is the first time the NRL has fully committed to playing Premiership games there regularly.

Pacific Islands dominate the 2021 World Cup

The 2021 Rugby League World Cup was delayed by an entire year due to the impacts of the coronavirus pandemic, yet despite being played in 2022, it was still regarded as the 2021 World Cup. The pandemic hit England very hard throughout 2021, so much that Australia and New Zealand announced that they would not risk their players by sending them to England to participate. World Cup organisers feared that the World Cup without those two nations would lack credibility, so they decided to delay the tournament until the following year.

The World Cup was the first to have the mens, women's and wheelchair World Cups all played concurrently for the first time. Seven of the 16 competing nations were from the Pacific region and six of those sides advancing to the finals. Australia defeated Samoa in the final, New Zealand reached the semi final while Tonga, Fiji and Papua New Guinea all reached the Quarter Finals. The Cook Islands were the only Pacific nation to miss the finals after winning one of their three Group games.

The Rise of Tonga and Samoa

The 2017 World Cup saw the rise of the Tonga on the International stage, as they advanced to the final four after winning all of their group games, including a 28–22 victory over New Zealand. They beat Lebanon 24–22 in the Quarter Finals, before losing to England 20–18 in a controversial semi-final. In 2019 Tonga beat Great Britain 14–6 and then Australia 16–12 a week later. Tonga advanced to the finals again in the 2021 World Cup before they fell short of the final again, this time to Samoa.

Samoa's turn around in the 2021 World Cup was unbelievable. They lost their opening game to England 60–6, but then beat Greece 72–4 and France 62–4 to sneak into the Finals. They then beat Tonga 20–18 and then England 27–26 to reach their first ever World Cup final, where they lost to Australia 30–10.

Australian Rugby League Hall of Fame

Inducted	Player
2002	Graeme Langlands
2002	Wally Lewis
2002	Clive Churchill
2002	John Raper
2002	Reg Gasnier
2002	Bob Fulton
2003	Mal Meninga
2003	Arthur Beetson
2003	Wally Prigg
2003	Dally Messenger
2003	Dave Brown
2003	Keith Holman
2004	Norm Provan
2004	Harold Horder
2004	Frank Burge
2004	Ken Irvine
2004	Vic Hey
2004	Harry Bath
2005	Duncan Thompson
2005	Ron Coote
2005	Brian Carlson
2005	Brian Bevan
2005	Chris McKivat
2005	Jim Craig
2006	Charles Fraser
2006	Sandy Pearce
2006	Duncan Hall
2006	Ken Kearney
2006	Peter Sterling
2006	George Treweek
2007	Arthur Halloway
2007	Keith Barnes
2007	Michael Cronin
2007	Harry Wells
2007	Tom Gorman
2007	Joe Pearce
2008	Frank McMillan
2008	Peter Madsen
2008	Jack Beaton
2008	Arthur Clues
2008	Joe Busch
2008	Andy Norval
2008	Viv Thicknesse
2008	Ernie Norman
2008	Ray Stehr
2008	Herb Narvo
2008	Ed Courtney
2008	Roy Bull
2008	Ian Walsh
2008	Les Johns
2008	Brian Hambly
2008	Eddie Lumsden
2008	Johnny King
2008	Barry Muir
2008	Noel Kelly
2008	John Sattler
2008	Brian Clay
2008	Bob McCarthy
2008	John O'Neill
2008	Kel O'Shea
2008	Brian Davies
2008	Ken Thornett
2008	Peter Gallagher
2008	Steve Walters
2008	Graham Eadie
2008	Brett Kenny
2008	Eric Grothe
2008	Kerry Boustead
2008	Gene Miles
2008	Steve Roach
2008	Wayne Pearce
2008	Brad Fittler
2008	Andrew Ettingshausen
2008	Andrew Johns
2008	Glenn Lazarus
2008	Allan Langer
2008	Bradley Clyde
2008	Laurie Daley
2008	Shane Webcke
2008	Darren Lockyer
2008	Terry Lamb
2008	Steve Rogers
2008	Tom Raudonikis
2008	Dan Dempsey
2008	Cec Blinkhorn
2008	Herb Steinohrt
2008	Howard Hallett
2008	Charles Fraser
2008	Les Cubitt
2008	Billy Smith
2008	Eric Weissel
2008	Herb Gilbert
2008	Billy Cann
2008	Albert Rosenfeld
2008	Dan Frawley
2008	Steve Mortimer
2008	Benny Wearing
2008	Vic Armbruster
2008	Ray Price
2008	Viv Farnsworth
2018	Ricky Stuart
2018	Cliff Lyons
2018	Steve Menzies
2018	Mark Graham
2018	Gorden Tallis
2018	Petero Civoniceva
2019	Stacey Jones
2019	Craig Young
2019	Ruben Wiki
2019	Danny Buderus
2019	James J. Giltinan
2019	Peter Frilingos
2019	Ray Warren
2023	George Piggins
2023	Ian Heads
2024	Lionel Morgan
2024	Les Boyd
2024	Ben Elias
2024	Steve Renouf
2024	Cameron Smith
2024	Johnathan Thurston
2024	Billy Slater
2024	Benji Marshall
2024	Cooper Cronk
2024	Greg Inglis
2024	Sam Burgess
2024	Natalie Dwyer
2024	Katrina Fanning
2024	Tarsha Gale
2024	Veronica White
2024	Karyn Murphy
2024	Tahnee Norris
2024	Frank Hyde
2024	Ken Arthurson
2024	John Quayle
2024	David Morrow
2024	Jack Gibson
2024	Wayne Bennett
2024	Col Pearce
2024	Bill Harrigan

Hall of Fame Key:

Mens | Womens | Coaches | Referees | Contributors

Premiership Records 1908–2018

Most Premierships

Club	Titles
South Sydney	21
St George*	15
Sydney Roosters	15
Balmain*	11
Canterbury	8
Manly	8
Brisbane	6 #
Penrith	6
Western Suburbs*	4
Parramatta	4
Melbourne	4 +
Newtown*	3
Canberra	3
North Sydney*	2
Newcastle	2
Wests Tigers	1
St George Illawarra	1
North Queensland	1
Cronulla	1

* defunct clubs

includes 1997 Super League title

+ Melbourne was stripped of the 2007 and 2009 titles due to salary cap breaches.

Biggest Wins in a Club Game

Year	Winner	Score	Opponent
1935	St George	91–6	Canterbury
1935	Easts	87–7	Canterbury
2003	North Qld	74–0	Wests Tigers
2003	Parramatta	74–4	Cronulla
1993	Canberra	68–0	Parramatta
1910	Souths	67–0	Wests

Top Try Scorers

Player	Years	Tries
Ken Irvine	1959–1973	212
Alex Johnston*	2014–2024	195
Billy Slater	2003–2018	190
Steve Menzies	1993–2008	180
Brett Morris	2006–2021	176
Andrew Ettingshausen	1983–2000	165
Terry Lamb	1980–1996	164
Daniel Tupou*	2012–2024	164
Brett Stewart	2003–2016	163
Hazem El Masri	1996–2009	159
Matt Sing	1993–2006	159
Josh Morris	2007–2021	158

* Still playing

Top Point Scorers

Player	Years	T	G	FG	Pts
Cameron Smith	2002–2020	48	1295	4	2786
Hazem El Masri	1996–2009	159	891	0	2418
Jarrod Croker	2009–2023	136	915	0	2374
Adam Reynolds*	2012–2024	50	1058	28	2344
Johnathan Thurston	2002–2018	90	923	16	2222
Andrew Johns	1993–2007	80	917	22	2176
Jason Taylor	1990–2001	47	942	35	2107
Darryl Halligan	1991–2000	80	855	4	2034

* Still playing

Most First Grade Games

Player	Years	Games
Cameron Smith	2002–2020	430
Cooper Cronk	2001–2019	372
Darren Lockyer	1995–2011	355
Terry Lamb	1980–1996	350
Steve Menzies	1993–2008	349
Paul Gallen	2001–2019	348
Corey Parker	2001–2016	347
Benji Marshall	2003–2021	346

Hazem El Masri.

Most Points in a Season

Player	Year	T	G	FG	Pts
Hazem El Masri	2004	16	139	0	342
Reuben Garrick	2021	23	121	0	334
Brett Hodgson	2005	15	124	0	308
Hazem El Masri	2006	17	114	0	296
Jarrod Croker	2016	18	112	0	296

Most Tries in a Season

Player	Year	T
Dave Brown	1935	38
Ray Preston	1954	34
Alex Johnston	2021	30
Alex Johnston	2022	30
Les Brennan	1954	29

Most Points in a Game

Player	Year	T	G	FG	Pts	Game details
Dave Brown	1935	5	15	0	45	Easts 87–7 v Canterbury
Dave Brown	1935	6	10	0	38	Easts 65–10 v Canterbury
Mal Meninga	1990	5	9	0	38	Canberra 66–4 v Easts
Jack Lindwall	1947	6	9	0	36	St George 61–11 v Manly
Terry Campese	2008	4	10	0	36	Canberra 74–12 v Penrith
Les Griffin	1935	2	15	0	36	St George 91–6 v Canterbury

Most Tries in a Game

Player	Year	Tries	Game details
Frank Burge	1920	8	Glebe 41–0 v University
Rod O'Loan	1935	7	Easts 61–5 v Univeristy

Australian International Records 1908–2024

Record All Internationals

Opponent	Played	Won	Lost	Draw
New Zealand	141	104	3	34
Great Britain	137	72	5	60
France	60	44	2	14
England	25	16	2	7
Wales	13	13	0	0
Papua New Guinea	11	11	0	0
Fiji	8	8	0	0
Samoa	5	5	0	0
Italy	3	3	0	0
South Africa	3	3	0	0
Tonga	3	3	0	0
Lebanon	2	2	0	0
Scotland	2	2	0	0
Ireland	1	1	0	0
Russia	1	1	0	0
Tonga Invitational	1	0	0	1
USA	1	1	0	0

Biggest Wins

Year	Score	Opponent
2000	110–4	Russia
2022	84–0	Scotland
2000	82–0	Papua New Guinea
1995	86–6	South Africa
1994	74–0	France
2003	76–4	Wales
1996	84–14	Fiji

Top Try Scorers

Player	Years	Tries
Ken Irvine	1959–1970	40
Darren Lockyer	1997–2011	37
Greg Inglis	2006–2016	31
Reg Gasnier	1959–1967	28
Billy Slater	2008–2017	27
Bob Fulton	1968–1978	26

Internationals for Australia

Player	Years	Games
Darren Lockyer	1997–2011	63
Cameron Smith	2006–2017	56
Mal Meninga	1982–1994	47
Graeme Langlands	1963–1975	45
Petero Civoniceva	2001–2011	45
Brad Fittler	1991–2001	40
John Raper	1959–1968	40
Reg Gasnier	1959–1967	39
Greg Inglis	2006–2016	39
Clive Churchill	1948–1956	38
Cooper Cronk	2007–2017	38
Johnathan Thurston	2006–2017	38
Bob Fulton	1968–1978	37

Top Point Scorers

Player	Years	T	G	FG	Pts
Johnathan Thurston	2006–2017	13	165	0	382
Mick Cronin	1973–1982	10	140	0	310
Mal Meninga	1982–1994	22	99	0	282
Andrew Johns	1995–2006	12	86	0	220
Darren Lockyer	1997–2011	37	29	3	209
Graeme Langlands	1963–1975	20	73	0	206
Michael O'Connor	1986–1990	17	65	0	198
Cameron Smith	2006–2017	9	67	0	170
Mat Rogers	1998–2000	9	66	0	168

Most Tries in an International for Australia

Player	Year	Tries	Game Details
Valentine Holmes	2017	6	Australia 54–6 v Fiji
Valentine Holmes	2017	5	Australia 46–0 v Samoa
Josh Addo-Carr	2022	5	Australia 48–4 v Lebanon

Most Tries in a Test

Player	Year	Tries	Game details
Valentine Holmes	2017	6	Australia 54–6 v Fiji
Valentine Holmes	2017	5	Australia 46–0 v Samoa
John Ribot	1982	4	Australia 38–2 v Papua New Guinea
Dale Shearer	1986	4	Australia 52–0 v France
Michael O'Connor	1988	4	Australia 70–8 v Papua New Guinea
Brett Dallas	1996	4	Australia 84–14 v Fiji
Gordon Tallis	2000	4	Australia 82–0 v Papua New Guinea
Mat Rogers	2000	4	Australia 66–8 v Fiji
Wendell Sailor	2000	4	Australia 110–4 v Russia
Brett Morris	2013	4	Australia 62–0 v USA
Jarryd Hayne	2013	4	Australia 62–0 v USA

Below: Australia's successful 1977 World Cup squad.

Basic Rules of Rugby League

The game is played by two teams over 80 minutes, split into two 40 minute halves. Each team has 13 players on the field, with an additional 4 available as interchange players. The object of the game is to score more points than your opponents, either by scoring tries, kicking goals or field goals.

Scoring values

Try = 4 points
Goal = 2 points
Field goal (within 40m of the posts) = 1 point
Field goal (from 40m or more away from the posts) = 2 points

Tries

A try is scored by placing the ball on the ground in the opponent's in-goal area.

Goals

There are only two ways to get an opportunity to kick a goal. After a try has been scored, a team then gets an opportunity to convert the try with a goal; or if a team receives a penalty, they can choose to have a kick at goal.

Field Goal

A field goal is a drop-kick at goal during play. A drop-kick is performed by dropping the ball to the ground and kicking it immediately after it bounces. A field goal is awarded when a drop kick passes over the crossbar and between the posts at the opponent's end of the field.

The Scrum

A scrum is formed to restart the game after a kick has gone into touch, a ball has been knocked on or a forward pass has been thrown. Six players from each side are used to form the scrum while a seventh player places the ball into the scrum.

Forward Pass

A forward pass happens when a pass is deliberately thrown forward to a team mate. Because players are moving at speed, however, passes may travel forward relative to the supporting player's movement but the pass must be thrown backward out of the hands.

Knock On

The ball is propelled forward by a player's hand or arm. A ball can be 'knocked on' in the air or on the ground, or into another player.

Kick-off

The game is started in each half and restarted after scoring plays by a kick. The ball is placed on the halfway line and must be kicked at least 10 metres forward. All players on the kicker's side must remain behind halfway line until after the ball has been kicked.

Obstruction

Obstruction is when a player is blocked from taking part in the game by a player without the ball. This is also known as 'shepherding'.

Tackling

A tackle is effectively completed when the player with the ball has their momentum stopped, either while still standing or by being brought to the ground. Tackles cannot strike above the shoulders, or be made using an intentional shoulder charge.

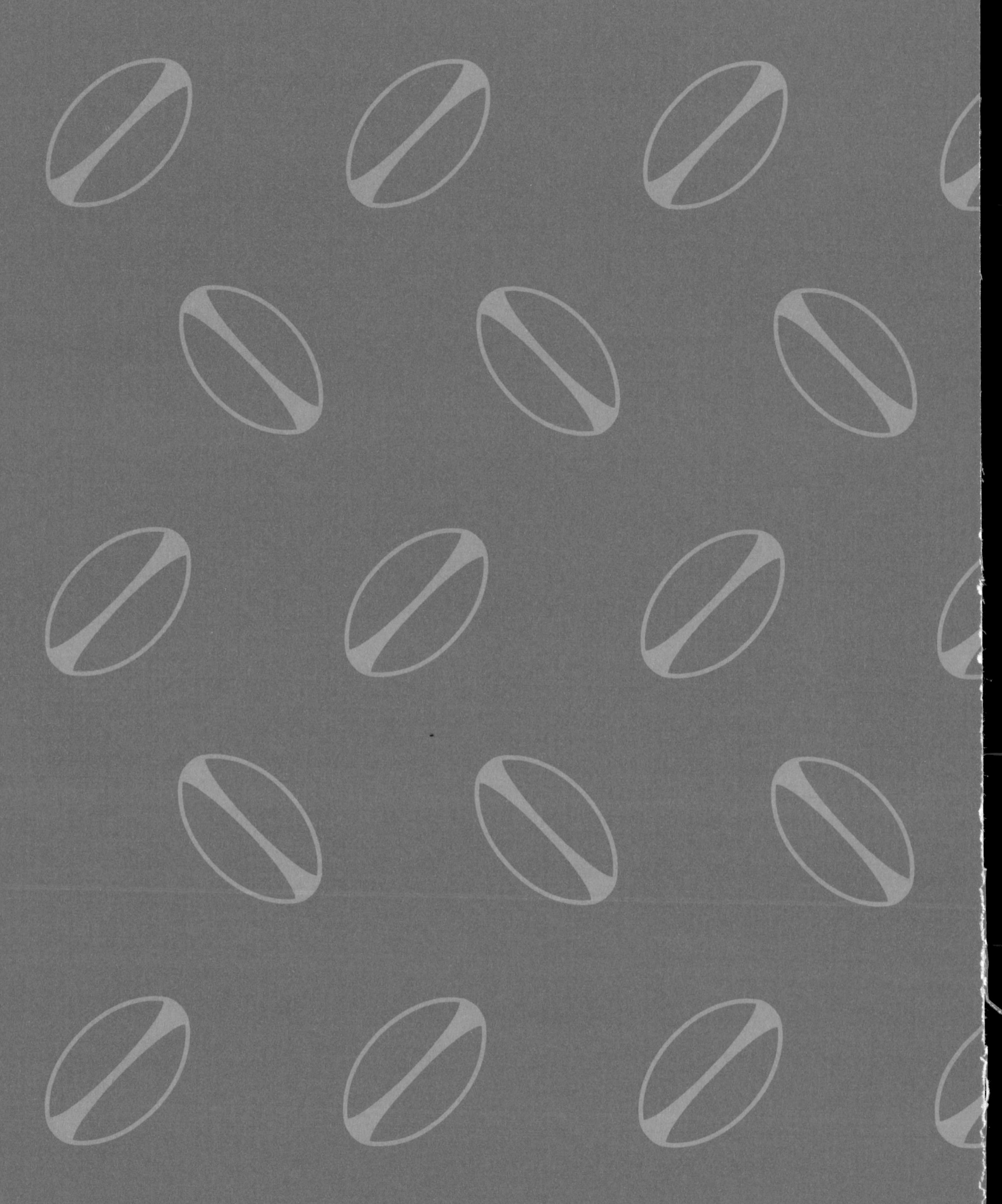